CONTENTS

GENGHIS KHAN
AND THE MONGOL EMPIRE

Jean-Paul Roux

DISCOVERIES®
HARRY N. ABRAMS, INC., PUBLISHERS

"And he said to them, 'My Lords, if you wish me to be your King, you shall swear to me by Him who made Heaven and earth to keep my commands.' And this they swore. The laws which he gave them were designed to keep the people at peace.... He gave them many other good laws for the keeping of the peace."

John of Joinville,
regarding Genghis Khan,
in *The Life of St. Louis*, 1955

CHAPTER 1
GENGHIS KHAN

No authentic portrait of Genghis Khan exists (opposite, Chinese painting on silk), but the fascination he elicited meant that his successors, the Yüans of China and the Il-khans of Iran, created many representations of him. Numerous objects have been considered his relics, like these stirrups (right), which so beautifully evoke the era of the hordes.

They were not yet called the Mongols

Only a few among them bore that name. Chinese annals mention it for the first time in the 8th century, with respect to the nomads camping on the upper reaches of the Amur River. Others were known only by the names of their tribes. But they all spoke the same idiom, a language of the Altaic family, related to that of the Tungusic-Manchu and Turkic peoples, with whom they also shared a religion founded in the belief in a single god, eternal and all-powerful, from whom emanated a multitude of lesser gods, such as the Earth Mother, the codivinity of heaven. They were devoted to shamanism, a mystical belief that involved trances, communication with animal spirits who revealed the future, magical healing powers, and the care of the souls of the deceased and of sacrificial animals beyond the grave.

They did not yet live in what would become Mongolia but in present-day Manchuria. They left their territory often to engage in various military undertakings, even to establish or to participate in the foundation of vast empires that plagued the sedentary civilizations. The most ancient among these marauding nomads, the Hsiung-nu (Huns)—the "barbarians of the North"—attacked China from the 2nd century BC through the 3rd century AD, although their historical role there is unclear. At that time the Avars, whom the Chinese named "the swarming insects," were at the forefront of a new empire in 6th-century Russia and the Balkans, the Juan-Juan (402–553) dominated Mongolia, and then, at the turn of the 6th century AD, the Hephthalites, or the White Huns, launched themselves at Afghanistan and India, where they brought desolation.

The occupation of new territories

The Mongols began to leave their ancestral lands for good in the 10th century. One group of them, the

The art of the steppes has long been examined through the metalwork of the nomadic peoples of Eastern Europe, particularly the Scythians and their neighbors. It is clear now that their aesthetic influence extended to the Chinese and Siberian borders. The discoveries made in the tombs trapped in the ice in Mongolia and in the Altai range reveal that the nomads also expressed themselves with textiles, such as felt set off by silk and carpets of fine wool. Above: This felt carpet fragment found in Noin Ula in Mongolia depicts mythical birds and the "combat of animals," which does not actually describe a conflict but rather a sexual union between a predator and its prey, that is, the origins of the human species, a tribe, or clan.

Khitans, or *Khitai*—from which Cathay, the old name for China, is derived—invaded the northern regions of the Middle Kingdom and there founded the Liao dynasty that was destined to last until 1125 when they were chased out by the Juchen, known as the Jin in Chinese. Then under the name of the Kara-Khitai, or the Black Khitans, they went on to establish their Buddhist domination in the Muslim countries of central Asia. Other nomads entered into Mongolia. There they encountered the Turkic peoples, who came from the forests of Siberia, where they had settled many years ago, and who had now made the Mongolian territory their country. This land became the center of the vast T'u-chüeh (the Blue Turks) (552–744) and Uighur (744–840) empires, but

According to the Mongols, the universe is haunted by spirits (above, a demon of the Uighur era) that men must fight and control, especially when they die and their souls go to the beyond. Left: The proto-Mongol Khitans (the Liao of China) may have placed these gold, silver, and bronze masks with their impassive human features on the faces of the dead as a sort of ruse, even though these objects generally were given a zoomorphic look.

their numbers dwindled due to continued migration to the west. The Mongols merged with these different peoples, sometimes assimilating them or being assimilated by them, at times sharing their pastures with them. Properly speaking, the Mongols, whom the Chinese knew on the Amur, installed themselves in the region watered by the Onon River. Their neighbors to the west were the Märkit, who moved seasonally between Lake Baikal and the Selenga River; and to the east the Tatars dominated the valley of the Kerulen River; and to the southeast the Kereyid occupied the center of the gravity of the empires of the steppes: the upper Onon, the upper Selenga, and the valleys of the Tuul and the Orkhon Rivers. Farther away toward the west lived the Naiman at the sources of the Selenga and the Irtysh Rivers in the Tarbagatai. To the north of the Uighurs (in the basin of the Tarim) were the Qarluk, and, far to the east, the Öngüt pastured the length of the Great Wall of China. The Kereyid and Naiman appeared to be half-Turk and half-Mongol. The Märkit and Tatars were Mongol speakers, while the Qarluk and the Öngüt spoke Turkic. The latter had converted to Christianity and showed themselves to be observant; the Kereyid had the reputation of being Christian but were so in name only.

Camels served commerce and horses the hunt and war. For migrations the Mongols used ox carts (*tereg*), described by travelers since the Middle Ages. An ancient one (bottom) was discovered in Pazyryk in the Altai. With their large wheels, the ox carts were able to handle all kinds of grazing lands. Below: A map of eastern Asia.

Their steppes were the most beautiful in the world

In the north was a peneplain, a land surface of considerable area slightly shaped by erosion, 4,900 to 5,300 feet (1,500 to 1,600 meters) high, blocked by mountains whose streaming waters were venerated for their life-giving quality. Existence, admittedly, was tough with temperatures

averaging 32°F (0°C) and with extremes ranging from over 100°F to –40°F (40°C to –40°C). Nature was generous. In the mountains grazed cattle and yaks; in the plains were sheep, goats, and horses numbering in the millions. In the south stretched the rocky Gobi desert, domain of the two-humped Bactrian camels used primarily by the nomads traveling from China to Iran.

The peoples of Mongolia usually lived in anarchy when there was no leader to impose his will and unite them. They were not unhappy in this state, but waited for someone who would stop their internal conflicts and lead them to a great destiny. The Mongols believed that this leader would be found at the end of the 11th century or at the beginning of the 12th, and they would be given an emperor—a khan, or *qaghan*. But because of their clashes with the Tatars and the Jin of the north of China, among others, their attempt at greatness came to a sudden end and the budding empire crumbled by 1161 at the latest. They didn't stop hoping.

They wished for a leader and, as this barbaric and uncultivated race was full of energy and endowed with a great spirit, this leader must prove to be an extraordinary

Above: Only great occasions brought families and clans together; most of the time Mongols lived in small units far from one another. Yurts, tents with a collapsible lattice framework covered with felt and with a hemispherical roof, were pitched in a clearing. Covering 65 to 72 square feet (18 to 20 square meters), they did not need to be fastened to the ground and they resisted even the harshest weather. These veritable microcosms of life obeyed strict rules of organization inside the yurt, while outside grazed sheep, bovines, and Bactrian camels.

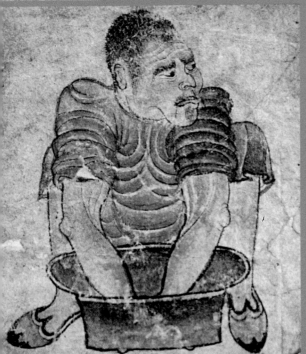

The great Turkish artist Mehmet Siyah Kalem (*Mehmet*, "black pencil") lived in central Asia in the 15th century. Using shades of black and somber tones enhanced with touches of red and gold, he painted scenes of worlds visible and invisible. His ungainly characters—muscular, thick-jointed, and moored to the ground—were represented with an acute sense of observation and audacity. This celebrated depiction of a nomadic camp includes, in addition to the expressive faces of the crouching men, a pack of raw-boned dogs and the almost surrealistic twisting in the legs and head of a horse eating a large flower.

personality, one of those men whom history does not produce more than once or twice a millennium.

A child named Temüjin

And so there was born—the exact date is unclear, perhaps in 1155, perhaps later—a little boy named Temüjin. His father, Yesügei, was the head of the Kiyat subclan of the Borjigin clan, a man who managed to ally himself by a fraternity of blood—a "sworn brotherhood"—to someone of a much higher station: Togrul,

The myth of the ancestral wolf, already well attested to by the Turks of the 6th and 7th centuries, reappeared among the Mongols as the first myth of the origin of Genghis Khan. In one story he was descended from a gray-blue wolf and a brown doe; and then in another where the wild creature is compared to the celestial

head of the Kereyid. His mother, Hö'elün, a female leader, came from the Märkit tribe from whom she was taken by force. Temüjin came from a good family, even if not one of the most important. The myth that would develop surrounding his birth attributed to him a twofold supernatural origin: he was descended from the offspring of a gray-blue wolf and a brown doe and had as a more recent ancestor Alan Qo'a, a woman impregnated by a ray of light. The legend would add that he was related to the ancient khans of the Mongols. His childhood was less auspicious, however, even though *The Secret History of the Mongols*, the annals of the origins of the Genghis-khanite dynasty, described him as having "fire in his eyes, with light in his face."

At a very early age he was engaged to a little girl, Börte, known as "the Cerulean one," who would herself develop into a formidable personality. Temüjin was still young, eight or nine years old, when his father was assassinated by the Tatars. His mother, his three brothers, his sister,

light that comes to fertilize Alan Qo'a. The two stories, particularly the second, were well mined by all sources. Here are two very different illustrations: the one (above left) is an abstract taken from *Subj-I-Panjane*, a 15th-century Timurid manuscript; the other (above right) is a more contemporary and realistic depiction. It is easy to discern both Christian and Greek influences in the myth of Alan Qo'a. The story surrounding Olympias, the mother of Alexander the Great, is perfectly in line with the traditions of central Asia, where it is not an isolated example.

and a former concubine of Yesügei and her two children were expelled from the clan. Condemned to lead an errant existence they fed themselves on garlic and wild onions, killed birds with small bows, and caught fish. Eventually defeated by hunger, they came to blows over the merest morsels and, in the end, one of them lost their life.

In quest of a clan, in search of status

But they survived and they grew. They were not outlaws, only outcasts, and they developed useful relationships. Temüjin's strong personality earned him friends, such as Bo'orchu, who remained faithful, and Jamuqa, who became his sworn brother but who betrayed Temüjin and eventually was killed by him. Temüjin's forceful nature would also bring him enemies who feared his charisma and said, "The little brats have grown." Temüjin was hunted. He fell into the hands of several abductors but displayed all his wits and deployed a thousand ruses to liberate himself. He dreamed of his father and of the alliances he had woven long ago. The Mongols were a faithful lot who

Below: This 16th-century Persian manuscript shows that the artist worked according to the conventions of his craft and the times. The illustrator has Islamicized the characters in this episode depicting the pursuit by Genghis Khan's mother of the clan that abandoned her.

generally respected a pledge. Couldn't he call upon the men of the past?

Temüjin resolved to seek the father of his childhood fiancée. He was well received by the Qongirat clan, who had never stopped considering him as a future son-in-law. The marriage was celebrated, and Temüjin finally achieved status through his in-laws. Then he dared to pay a visit to Togrul the Kereyid, his father's sworn brother, who told him, "I will reunite your scattered people. I will bring together your family." It was a promise to act and Togrul soon had to prove his sincerity. Shortly thereafter the Märkit abducted Börte, and Temüjin was reduced to fleeing and hiding in the Burqan Qaldun, now known as the Kentei Mountains, or the Hentiyn Nuruu. Although they searched for him, they could not find Temüjin. The mountain had protected him. Every day from then on, he said, he prayed to the divinity enthroned in the mountain; every day he would offer up a sacrifice.

Temüjin is proclaimed khan

Togrul and Jamuqa, his sworn brother, convened their men to free the young woman. They overcame the Märkit and freed Börte. Several months later when she

The meeting of the Kereyid leader Togrul and the future Genghis Khan is a key event in the life of the conquerer, according to historian Rashid ad-Din (1247–1318). The images from his encyclopedic *Jami al-Tawarikh* (*World History*) are more or less faithful to the events, based on the versions and the era. Above: Despite the Chinese influence expressed here in the writhing forms of the tree and the clouds, the illustrator shows a solid knowledge of yurts and local costumes.

gave birth to her firstborn, Jöchi, people did not seek to discover who was the father. Here was the last great proof. His clan rallied to Temüjin; the Mongol nobles and the powerful came as well. An assembly, or *khuriltai*, convoked around 1195–1196 and proclaimed him khan. Soon after Temüjin began to promulgate laws. Completed over the passage of time, they became the *Yasaq*, a political and moral code studded with ancestral traditions. This code, of which only fragments remain, would serve as the essential reference of governance and was practically sacred to his successors and to their people.

But his election created malcontents. Jamuqa, with whom relations were already strained, fell out with him. Allied with the Jin and the Kereyid, Temüjin battled against the Tatars in 1198 without deriving either glory or advantage. With only the Kereyid by his side, he abandoned an uncertain war against the Naiman in 1199. Finally in 1202, after several fruitless campaigns, he managed to crush the Tatars totally. He massacred some and recruited the majority, who were then often seen at the vanguard of his troops—a strange destiny for a people who were traditionally hostile to the Mongols. To the Tatars' great anger, their name in the form of "Tartar" would serve to designate not only the Mongols themselves but also, much later and in a more general fashion, all the nomads of the Eurasian steppes, especially those Turks who would not rebuild the Ottoman Empire.

His alliance with Togrul allowed the future Genghis Khan to vanquish his adversaries in Mongolia and, in particular, his sworn enemies the Tatars. Below: His pursuit culminated with the decapitation of their khan; a young woman—no doubt Börte, Temüjin's young wife—seated nonchalantly in the Oriental style on a sort of throne regards the scene complacently. The heads of the most important enemy chiefs often were used as trophies or cult objects.

The Turko-Mongols long believed that there could be only one emperor on earth just as there was only one god in heaven. In other words, Togrul the Kereyid and Temüjin the Mongol could not rule side by side. Their old friendship itself would not permit it. They confronted one another, and Togrul lost his life in 1203. Temüjin annexed Togrul's lands and his people and became the true master of eastern and central Mongolia. The Naiman no longer had power against him. They searched for an ally who could push the Mongols back

Above: Fortified cities were obstacles in the relentless march of the Mongol warriors who, at the time of their first advances, did not have siege machines. Their assaults began in northern China and against the cities of the southwest.

and thought they would find support among the Öngüt, but the Öngüt chose instead to warn Temüjin. Although they hoped to surprise him, it was the Naiman who were taken unawares. They collapsed with the first attack. He who would become Genghis Khan would never forget the favor shown to him by the Öngüt. A tradition of matrimonial alliances was inaugurated between the two tribes, and Temüjin gave them as well as their belief in Christianity a place of distinction in the empire.

Genghis Khan, the "oceanic sovereign"

Temüjin now controlled all of Mongolia. For the second time and with more solemnity, an assembly of tribal chiefs, the *khuriltai*, pro-claimed him emperor in 1206. It was at this time that Temüjin took the name *Tchingis Qaghan*—which translates as "oceanic sovereign"— from which Genghis Khan is derived. Mongolia was born. It was not the least important consequence of the Genghis-khanite saga.

All that remained was to conquer the world. Genghis Khan began prudently by defending his rear guard. In 1207 he sent his son Jöchi to subdue the forest dwellers of southern Siberia, who were always ready to attempt some raids on Mongolia. Then he attacked the Tangut, or Hsi-Hsia, who, in the southern Gobi, formed a sort of third China, next to that of the Jin and the Sung (1207–1208). Genghis Khan was satisfied with the Tanguts' tacit submission in principle and by the promise of their sovereign to join their troops to his when needed.

Almost at the same time Temüjin received unsolicited tributes from the Qarluk and the Uighurs. The latter, a people of an ancient and high culture from the Tarim basin (the current Xinjiang), entered his service. The Uighurs furnished him with their alphabet, which is still

Below: By referring to the court ceremonies of the dynasties founded by the Mongols in China and in Iran, painters liked to represent Genghis Khan on a throne like a son of heaven or like a Muslim sultan. Along with their desire to become masters of the world, the Mongols developed a taste for pomp and splendor and loved to display their pre-dominance. The carefully established hierarchical order was evidence of the total power of the universal *qaghan*, and the numerous rites celebrat-ing his personality did not suffer in comparison to those observed for the great monarchs of seden-tary cultures.

in use among the Mongols, and were an indispensable part of the framework of the administration of the empire. Others followed them a little later, like those Khitans who had not traversed upper Asia with the Kara-Khitai and who now rallied to Genghis Khan.

In the conquest of China...

The nomads of Mongolia began their conquests by attacking China. In March 1211 Genghis Khan declared war on the kingdom of the Jin, which dominated the north of the country. Even though he had prepared his offensive with great care, he made no headway for some two years on the Chinese borders at the foot of the Great Wall. He took advantage of the slow progress to occupy Manchuria, a territory of about 386,000 square miles (1,000,000 square kilometers). Finally in 1215 he overwhelmed Peking (Beijing), which caused a great sensation. Having a premonition that the war would drag on, Genghis Khan left the command of his troops to his lieutenant Muqali in 1217 and returned to Mongolia. Almost immediately, he dispatched one of his best generals, Jebe, in the conquest of the realm of the Kara-Khitai, who had given asylum to deserters from Mongolia and where, he claimed, they conspired against him. In this Muslim country that was, or believed itself to be, oppressed by the Buddhists, the Mongols were received as liberators.

Below left: At some 2,300 miles (6,000 kilometers), the Great Wall of China's present form includes a complex array of fortifications rebuilt during the Ming era (14th–15th centuries), but the first unified wall has existed from the 3rd century BC. For the Mongols led by Genghis Khan (below right, practically caricatured by a Chinese illustrator), the wall remained an obstacle before which they toiled for many years.

Left: This Iranian miniature refers to Genghis Khan's victory over the emperor of China, but the exact meeting is unclear. The mountainous landscape—which may have been imagined by the artist—is reminiscent of a narrow gorge in which a battle took place in 1213. There the Mongol forces were commanded by Tolui, the youngest son of the khan. The fall of Peking in 1215 had a global impact, which was a culmination of the fighting that preceded it. However, the most bloody battle had already taken place in the spring of 1211. The ground remained strewn with cadavers for so long that the Taoist monk Ch'ang-ch'un is said to have seen them nine years later. Genghis Khan himself led the army in China from 1211 to 1217 but did not conquer the great city. Complete domination was only achieved long after him in 1280 by his grandson Kublai Khan.

...and Iran

The Mongols were along the banks of the Syr Darya on the borders of Iran, which was still in the hands of Ala ad-Din Muhammad, shah of Khwarezm. Despite his reputation as being cowardly and ineffective, Muhammad had succeeded in gathering under his authority Afghanistan and Sogdiana, in addition to Iran. He appeared powerful but, in reality, his empire was too new and lacked cohesion. It would not be impossible to bring him down. A tragic incident concerning a caravan stopped in 1218 at Otrar on the Syr Darya on the Iranian frontier became the pretext for war. Muhammad dispersed his army while Genghis Khan gathered some 150,000 to 200,000 men. In September 1219 Genghis

Khan crossed the river and penetrated into Sogdiana.
In January 1220 he reached Bukhara, which capitulated
on February 15. In March he entered Samarkand. The
Mongols destroyed more or less everything in their path,
though they spared the artisans and all the members of
the Muslim clergy, honoring a respect for holy men of
all faiths. This move undermined Muhammad's
credibility a great deal when he later preached holy war
against the Mongols. The shah panicked. He resisted
no longer but abandoned his soldiers and fled. Jebe and
Subotai were sent in pursuit with 20,000 horsemen.
They followed him to Bactra (now Balkh), Nishapur,
Rey (Tehran), and Qazvin. Muhammad was not captured.
He would die of fear, of despair, and of exhaustion on a
little island in the Caspian Sea in December 1220 or
January 1221.

Across Afghanistan and as far as the Indus Valley

South of the Amu Darya, Jalal ad-Din Mingburnu, the
son of Shah Muhammad, pursued the battle. He took
up the offensive again and chased the Mongols out of
Sogdiana. Genghis Khan hesitated. Perhaps he was afraid
to commit so early. He decided to go ahead knowing full
well that he had no other means to assure his victory
than to render it complete. And so a terrible cataclysm
descended upon eastern Iran and Afghanistan through

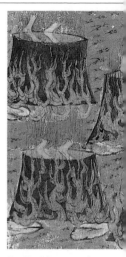

More than any other area, the region of eastern Iran endured countless Mongol assaults and still carries irreparable signs of destruction. Near Bamiyan, in the Hindu Kush, where two colossal statues of Buddha were raised, Genghis Khan's beloved grandson Mutugen perished in combat in 1221. The emperor, contrary to his custom, led the assault himself. Everything was destroyed. Left: Two ghost towns with their imposing vantage points, Chahr-I Golgola (City of Sighs) and Chahr-I Zohag (Red City), attest to the carnage. As in Merv, where they spoke of one or two million victims, one can say here that "not a head was left on a body."

Left: Even though they were perhaps exaggerated by propaganda, the destruction and massacres wrought by the Mongols were indeed terrible. They gave birth to all sorts of legends, which were not unfounded, such as this episode illustrated by Rashid ad-Din of prisoners thrown alive into boiling cauldrons. All means were used to sow terror.

Below: Jebe (here riding in front of Genghis Khan) had fought against the emperor before becoming

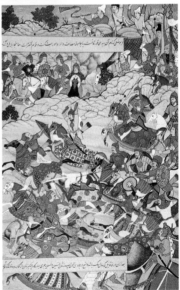

1221–1222. Cities were wiped out, whole populations were put to the sword. Sometimes everything was killed, including cats and dogs. In Merv (now Mary), there were reports of 700,000 dead. Near Bamiyan, in Afghanistan, two ghost towns still attest to the Mongol fury. On November 24, 1221, Jalal ad-Din Mingburnu, driven back to the Indus, abandoned the battle. His forces were vanquished but he escaped. Genghis Khan, however, had only won a half-victory. The loser rebuilt his empire with disconcerting speed and the Mongols had to destroy it anew. But Genghis Khan knew how far he could go; to undertake the conquest of India would be foolishness. A year later, when the Mongols besieged Multan (now in Pakistan), they were forced to withdraw, not being able to live in a stiflingly hot country.

Muhammad was dead and those who had hunted him found themselves in the remotest part of Iran. They began their return journey but did not choose the most direct route. Crossing the Caucasus Mountains, the

one of his best and most faithful generals.

Genghis Khan, like all good Turko-Mongols, was interested in religion. He learned about Islam and discussed it with his theologians. The Iranian historian 'Ala-ad-Din 'Ata-Malik Juvaini may not have been the most credible source when he wrote that the emperor gathered together all the Muslims in the Great Mosque of Bukhara and terrified them by presenting himself as the Scourge of God. Opposite: This 14th-century Persian miniature, which shows Genghis Khan in a garden seated on the steps of a *minbar* (prayer pulpit) orating like a Muslim *khatid* (preacher), may refer to the episode described by Juvaini. In 1220 Bukhara was the first city the emperor entered (he disdained visiting Peking) and the great and prosperous city made a strong impression on him. He was merciful toward them although, admittedly, there were summary executions and no doubt massacres, but there was no systematic extermination of the inhabitants. A fire—probably accidental—destroyed a large part of the city, which now retains only two edifices built prior to the blaze. Left: This late-16th-century Mughal Indian miniature depicts a magnificent city, but one whose architecture, rugs, and clothes are far from medieval reality.

Mongol warriors were forced to challenge the Georgians, then at the height of their glory after the reigns of David the Confessor (1089–1129) and Queen Thamar (1184–1213). They emerged onto the plains of the Ukraine, which was in the hands of the Kipchak Turks, also known as the Polovtsi by the Russians or the Cumans by the Hungarians. Judging themselves incapable of confronting Jebe and Subotai alone, the Kipchaks called for the help of the Russian princes. They arrived, arrogant, undisciplined, jealous of each other, and were squashed at the Kalka River. The beginning of the *tatartchina*—the subjugation of the Russians by the Tatars—dates generally from May 31, 1222. Jebe and Subotai then skirted the Caspian Sea from the north, pushed around the Bulgars of the Volga, and rejoined Genghis Khan in the heart of central Asia after having traveled about 12,500 miles (20,000 kilometers) in four years and having vanquished five great peoples. They had lived a saga that had never before been experienced and would never be repeated.

A final campaign

Genghis Khan was growing older but he did not want to die. He had heard tell that the Taoists possessed a medicine for immortality and summoned one of their masters, Ch'ang-ch'un, who crossed upper Asia to see him in 1222. He told him that there were indeed ways to prolong life—not to render it eternal—and admonished him to renounce all pleasures, the hunt, licentiousness, and drunkenness. Genghis Khan listened but did not protest, and lavished his guest with attention. Then slowly—he never hurried—he started back for Mongolia and arrived there in 1225. He was weary. A riding accident had hurt and fatigued him. He had to rest, but he wanted to punish the Tangut, who had promised but failed to rally to him. In the course of the winter of 1225–1226, Genghis Khan crossed the Gobi and marched

Like all of his people, Genghis Khan was an expert horseman and devoted himself to the hunt, which had recreational, economic, and symbolic meaning, and served as an apprenticeship for future warriors. The sport was practiced individually or collectively and expeditions kept the hunters out for weeks. Opposite: Hunters avoided spilling blood, which was supposed to contain the animal's soul, and used methods such as traps, stoning, strangulation by lasso, or even falcons. His passion for hunting eventually led the emperor to his death. He was hurt for the first time in March 1223 by falling from a horse during an expedition. In vain, they tried to divert his attention from the pastime. Weakened or just aging, he had a second fall in autumn 1225 that was so serious his entourage suggested that he interrupt his war against the Tangut.

against them. He felt invincible. He defeated the Tangut, but he died shortly after—perhaps on August 12, 1227—before seeing them capitulate. In honor of his Manes (the deified spirits of the dead honored with graveside sacrifices), there was an immense slaughter of the vanquished Tangut. A slow and somber procession brought back his body to Mongolia.

Not wanting to renounce either the hunt or war, Genghis Khan died in 1227 as a consequence, by his own admission, of a hunting accident. Opposite: His funeral rites were superb.

Genghis Khan unified the Mongols and founded an empire, but it remained for his successors to continue his quest for there to be only one sovereign on earth as there is only one god in heaven. Led by princes of genius, they would wage war in China, Korea, Southeast Asia, Iran, India, the Near East, Russia, and eastern Europe, displaying an intense diplomatic activity. For more than half a century, the Mongols would make the East and the West tremble.

CHAPTER 2
THE SUCCESSORS

The investiture of the *qaghans* was accompanied by a precise ceremony. Opposite: For Ögödei's in 1229, the texts relate that his uncle, holding his left hand, his brother Chagatai his right hand, and Tolui his belt, led him to the throne and offered him a cup, and that all the assistants were on bended knee. Right: An image of Kublai, the Grand Khan and emperor of China.

The new emperor had to be elected by a plenary assembly as Genghis Khan had been, but the chosen one must be from the same bloodline as the late sovereign. Reuniting all the electors dispersed to the four corners of the empire took time. The interregnum was punctuated occasionally by the regencies of leaders such as Tolui (1227–1229), youngest son of Genghis Khan, nicknamed "Prince of Fire" (*otchigin*) because he was responsible for guarding the paternal hearth—his father's original territory of the region between the Tuul, upper Onon, and upper Kerulen Rivers. Later imperial widows such as Töregene (1242–1246) and Oghul Qaimish (1248–1251) ruled the land. History has judged that these leaders proved themselves worthy of the task. The first elected sovereigns following the death of Genghis Khan, Ögödei (1229–1241), Güyük (1246–1248), and Mangu (also known as Mongka) (1251–1259), also proved to

In 1258 Mangu, the third successor to Genghis Khan, who had ruled for seven years, reprised the Mongol offensive on China. He entered into Sichuan, captured several cities, and was stopped in front of Ho-tcheou (Ho-ts'iuan). Afflicted by dysentery, Mangu died in April 1259 outside the city walls. Ho-tcheou was later captured by Mangu's brother and successor Kublai, Grand Khan and founder of the Yüan dynasties. Below: The illustration shows hand-to-hand combat between defenders and attackers in front of the city.

Left: Tolui (1193–1232), represented here with his family in a 14th-century Persian miniature from the *Jami al-Tawarikh* (*World History*) by Rashid ad-Din, was the youngest son of Genghis Khan. According to the Turko-Mongol tradition, it was incumbent on Tolui to remain in the paternal lands, which earned him the right to carry the title of *otchigin*, or "Prince of Fire." His influence was considerable. He was charged with the regency (1227–1229) after his father's death; two of his sons, Mangu and Kublai, would become grand khans; another, Hülegü, the viceroy of Iran, founded the Il-khan dynasty there. He was married to a Nestorian Christian woman of exceptional talents, the Kereyid Sorghaqtani, and as a consequence all his sons favored Christianity. The death of Tolui, due without a doubt to alcoholism, was considered a self-sacrifice destined to save the life of the reigning *qaghan* who was menaced by the "sovereigns and the lords of the earth and the water"—the lands of China. This very famous legend led to the placing of a proscription on the name of the dead prince.

be dignified heirs of their father and grandfather, furthering his military and political work.

An excessive expansion of the empire…

For thirty years the Mongols experienced victory after victory and succeeded in greatly expanding the empire. They conquered Korea between 1231 and 1236, though it was necessary later to intervene there several times to reestablish order. Tibet, whose own version of its history suggests that it rallied to the Mongols around 1206–1207, was in fact annexed around 1250, and its monks did not delay in exercising a strong influence on the Mongols, which lessened through the years. The war that Genghis Khan had begun against northern China, the land of the Jin, was succeeded immediately by an interminable conflict against the Sung in southern China (1234–1279). The Mongols were incapable of operating as cavalrymen in these unfamiliar southern lands that were studded with cities and lacked pastures. The great Khitan minister Yeh-lü Ch'u-ts'ai, who became a counselor to Genghis Khan in 1215 but fell out of favor in 1244, dissuaded the Mongols from transforming these lands into steppes by destroying everything. (He convinced them that the taxes would be more profitable if the cities remained standing.) The Mongols therefore had to draw the Chinese to them and recruit them, and also adapt themselves in some ways to the Chinese, which demanded a prodigious effort. It was, of course, impossible for them at the same time to become Indians in order to conquer India, or turn into Bedouins in Syria and Egypt, or Franks in central and western

Europe, which was one of the essential reasons that the universal domination they sought would be limited.

In Iran, Jalal ad-Din Mingburnu reconstructed the kingdom of Khwarezm, and although he was an accomplished paladin, he succeeded in falling out with all the neighboring princes, including the Abbasid caliph of Baghdad. Mingburnu went on to lay waste to Georgia, although his own lands had not yet healed from the wounds occasioned by the Mongol raids of 1220–1221. In 1230–1231 several Mongol squadrons made a surprise attack on the country still paralyzed by fear and struck it a great blow. Only the city of Isfahan put up a strong resistance and paid dearly for it but, by some good fortune, the city's Seljuk architectural masterpieces were not destroyed.

After having marched against Novgorod in the spring of 1238, Batu withdrew toward the south and was stopped for seven weeks in Kozelsk within the borders of the present Ukraine. Above, from a 16th-century chronicle: The battle persevered. The city only capitulated when all of its defenders were massacred. The Russians would long remember the event.

In 1236 the Mongols compelled the Georgians, led by Queen Rusudan, to become vassals, then three years later the Armenians succumbed. If the former seemed not to accept their submission well, the latter suffered little as a result and quickly resigned themselves to it. The Armenians saw in their protectors the enemies of their enemy—Islam—and in return showed themselves to be skillful and servile subjects. In 1248 the Armenian high constable Sempad went to pay court to Güyük as a prelude to a voyage to Mongolia in 1254 by their king Hayton (also known as Hethum).

...up to the Ukraine

Contrary to the small army engaged in fighting in Iran, the one entrusted that same year (1236) to Batu, son of Jöchi, was considerable. Its mission was the conquest of western Europe—of the Kipchak, the Bulgars of the Volga, and the Russians, who had recently been vanquished. Given their way of life and their Turkic language, the Kipchaks and the Bulgars barely resisted rallying to the Mongols. Both peoples, but particularly the former, entered en masse into the Mongol army and into Batu's political apparatus to the point of making it almost a Turkic army and to the point of making it the formative state of the Golden Horde—the khanate of Kipchak. The Russians had other ideas, though they were no less quickly overwhelmed by the Mongols. Ryazan', Kolomna, Moscow, Vladimir, Suzdal'... succumbed one after the other, and if proud Novgorod in the north escaped invasion it was thanks only to the thawing ice that transformed the ground into quagmires (1238). Nevertheless, Novgorod had to pay taxes and receive the

King Hayton (Hethum) of Armenia (1226–1270) rallied enthusiasm for the Mongols, whom his people saw as the enemies of Islam. In 1248 he sent the high constable Sempad to the court of the conquerors, then went himself in 1254–1255 to meet Mangu in Karakorum. The details of the king's voyage and his remarkable observations were taken down by his historian Kirakos. Hayton then participated in the principal Mongol operations in the Near East, notably in Iraq and Syria. Below: A painting from *La Flore des estoires de la terre d'Orient*, written by his namesake, the monk Hayton, represents him here with the Grand Khan.

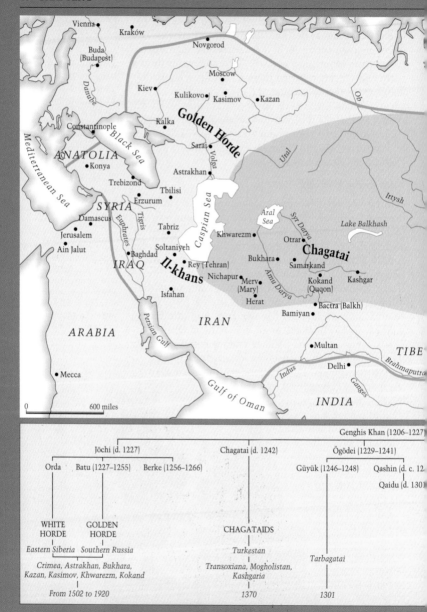

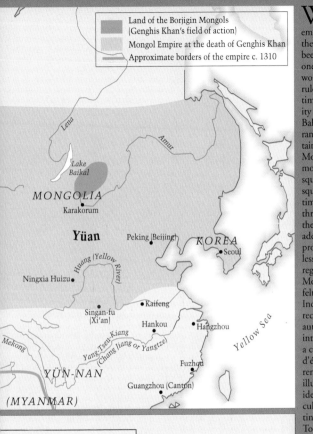

Land of the Borjigin Mongols (Genghis Khan's field of action)

Mongol Empire at the death of Genghis Khan

Approximate borders of the empire c. 1310

While there have been modern empires as vast as that of the Mongols, none has been ruled like it, all in one block. The ancient world was almost entirely ruled for the first and last time by the same authority from the Pacific to the Baltic and the Mediterranean. Despite the uncertain northern frontiers, the Mongol Empire covered more than 11,500,000 square miles (30,000,000 square kilometers), fifty times larger than France, three times larger than the United States. In addition, it exercised a protectorate—more or less direct—on many regions that bordered it. Mongol influence was felt even to the south of India, where the rajahs recognized the khan's authority. The division into four khanates (ulus), a consequence of a coup d'état by Kublai in 1260, rendered political unity illusory, but the same ideology and the same culture would long continue to inspire them all. Top: The map serves only as a rough guide because the frontiers of the Mongol Empire fluctuated and the exact layout is still a subject of discussion. Below this is a simplified genealogy of the Genghis-khanite rulers and their reigns.

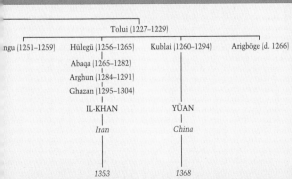

Tolui (1227–1229)

...ngu (1251–1259)	Hülegü (1256–1265)	Kublai (1260–1294)	Arigböge (d. 1266)
	Abaqa (1265–1282)		
	Arghun (1284–1291)		
	Ghazan (1295–1304)		
	IL-KHAN	YÜAN	
	Iran	China	
	1353	1368	

Above: One of Ögödei's most important decisions was to establish a city so that the empire had a capital just like fixed nations. Karakorum was situated in northern Mongolia on the banks of the Orkhon, a place that was always at the heart of the empire of the steppes. It was a modest town, and the Franciscan monk Rubruck judged that it was "worth less than the working class neighborhood of Saint-Denis" in Paris. Each ethnic group had its own neighborhood, each religion its temples. As for the palace, it had a basilican plan like the Seljuk caravansaries and Romanesque churches. Opposite, top: Among the vestiges found in situ are two enormous stone tortoises, images of the cosmos used for centuries, which supported inscribed steles. Opposite, bottom: The steppes are strewn with crude reliefs, which are difficult to date, representing rams and men. Left: The piles of plain stones erected near tombs represent slain enemies.

Mongol governor within its city walls. Once the northern and central Russian territories submitted, the hordes spread to the Ukraine, forcing it under their control (1239–1241).

Europe trembles

Refugees, fugitives, merchants, spies, propagandists all carried with them the news of the cataclysm that had struck the slavic world and they spread word of the terror to central and western Europe. Holy Roman Emperor and German king Frederick II spoke of the "cohorts of Satan" and the "children of hell." The German emperor understood that the Mongols "desired to rule over and dominate the surface of the world," and that everybody had reason to fear them. But could one believe that they would wage a war on Christianity? Beginning in the winter of 1241 the Mongols crossed the Vistula River, and thus began what would be the most impressive campaign of the Genghis-khanites. It led them across all of Poland (the taking of Kraków) and Silesia, where in Legnica (Liegnitz) in April the Teutonic cavalry was crushed in the Battle of Wahlstadt. The Mongols then marched against Hungary, took Buda (now part of Budapest), advanced to the gates of Vienna, traveled across Croatia and Dalmatia, and led their horses to

Ever since Bela III and his marriage to a Capetian princess, Hungary was the rising power in Europe, but it was not prepared for war against the Mongols despite all the warnings. Below: The nomad warriors rushed the Hungarian troops of Bela IV from hidden cover, forced them into the narrow gorges of the Carpathian Mountains, and massed their troops in front of Buda (Budapest) in April 1241. The Hungarians counterattacked immediately; the Mongols pretended to flee and then turned around to confront the Hungarians again at Mohi. The Mongols won a complete victory, one of the most brilliant in their history. That day also marked the greatest disaster in medieval chivalry. The Tartar cavalry spread across the *putszka*, the great plain, leaving it a ruin, crossed the Danube, took Zagreb, pressed on to Split, Kotor (Cattaro), and then Dubrovnik (also known as Ragusa). If nothing could have been more stunning than these victories, nothing could have been more useless; in 1242 the Mongols left central Europe, never to return.

yur un pone q la estoit mer le Due dautriche fist le pont gar

pelles wedn z fu le segonde fils de aurora.

Since the foundation of their order by Francis of Assisi, the Franciscans were everywhere, often at the peril of their lives. (Left: Their martyrdom at Ceuta in Morocco, from a work by the Italian painter Ambrogio Lorenzetti c. 1331.) They were the first to visit the Mongols after their European campaign, despite the terrifying rumors about them, largely spread by the German emperor Frederick II (below).

drink from the waters of the Adriatic Sea (1248). But they would go no further. It was not the death of Ögödei in December 1241 and the desire of the princes to participate in his successor's election that brought about the decline. Rather, it was the cumulative fatigue of the long campaigns, the relative smallness of the pastures on the Hungarian plains, and the impossibility of maneuvering the cavalry in the western forests. Slowly Batu withdrew toward the steppes. He was glad to return.

In the course of the winter of 1242–1243, the Mongols entered Asia Minor and vanquished the Seljuks on June 26. Instructed by Iran's example of not offering a useless resistance, they engaged in peace negotiations instead. They realized that their best hope was to be a protectorate, which at least would allow them their crown and the suggestion of sovereignty. Following this precedent the Greek king of Trebizond also hastened to be recognized a vassal.

Between diplomacy and the resumption of hostilities

The Christian West deemed it indispensable to have direct contact with the Mongols and to obtain more precise information about them. Italian Franciscan monk Giovanni da Pian del Carpini (in 1246–1247), French Franciscan friar Willem van Ruysbroeck (also known as William of Rubruck) (in 1253–1255), and several others started on great intercontinental voyages to discover Asia. They went first to the Near East, the Caucasus, Iran, and Mongolia, and later they would go to China (which Marco Polo, his father, and his uncle visited in 1275). Travelers would also profit from this opening of routes to go to India. In return the Mongols sent their ambassadors to the West. Oftentimes these men were Europeans who had entered the service of the Mongols, such as the Genovese Buscarel de Gisolf (from 1274–1307), and sometimes their own subjects, the most famous of whom was Rabban Bar Sauma (from 1287–1288), the Christian Öngüt monk born near Peking. They were seen in Rome, Lyons, Avignon, Paris, and Bordeaux.

The great diplomatic activity of the second half of the 13th century, marked by the creation of embassies and,

The missions were great events. Above: This 15th-century illustration depicts Kublai Khan sending a message to the pope via the Polo brothers.

moreover, by an important written exchange between the khans, the pope, and the Western kings, indicated a change in the comportment of the conquerors, perhaps hinting that the era of their great domination was nearing its end.

Mangu decided on the resumption of hostilities, which had fallen off. In 1253 he sent his brother Hülegü to Iran as a viceroy, where he would establish his own dynasty, the Il-khans; in China his brother Kublai, the future grand khan and founder of the Yüan dynasty, achieved results far beyond what had been accomplished before.

In India, after the successes of 1241 that rendered several rajahs as tributaries, there were vain attempts at offering resistance in 1257–1258, and control over the Kashmir was upheld by a new expedition around 1273. China would be, for the first time in its history, completely unified, though the domination of Southeast Asia was never well established. After the solid victory over Yün-nan in 1253, the battles for Tonkin (1257), Champa (1288), and Burma (now Myanmar) (1297) were to the contrary uncertain and precarious, and the Mongols would not be able either to land in Japan, despite two attempts in 1268 and 1271, or install themselves in Indonesia, where they failed after having set foot in Java in 1293.

After spectacular success in the Near East, things turned sour. In Iran the invincible hashish smokers, the Assassins—Shiite extremists who used murder for political means—

In response to the religious travelers who had been visiting them since 1245, the Mongols sent their own ambassadors to the papacy and to Western sovereigns with demands for them to submit. After their failure in Syria, they sought an alliance with the Franks and the tone of their letters changed. Many examples of these exchanges, both in the Mongol language and in Latin, have been preserved. Below: One of the most famous is from Khan Arghun of Iran to Philip the Good, Duke of Burgundy, which was carried on a diplomatic mission directed by Buscarel, a Genovese who had long been in the khan's service. It proposed a common offensive by the Mongols and the Crusaders on Damascus and promised that Jerusalem would be handed over to the king of France.

For a long time the Mongols knew nothing but military successes in Eurasia. Pages 50–51: The capture of Baghdad, the collapse and liquidation in 1256 of the Ismailian sect (also known as the hashish smokers, *haschischin,* or Assassins), and the destruction of the Abbasid caliphate plunged Islam into consternation. The capture of the "eagle's nests" from which they perpetrated their political crimes was no less of an exploit. (Left: The capture of Alamut.) Everyone united as a priority against terrorists but, despite all the efforts, no one had managed to get rid of them, except for the Mongols.

Trying to become sailors the Mongols attempted maritime operations against the great Asian islands of Indonesia (1293) and Japan, only to be met with bitter failure. (Pages 48–49: Scene of the Mongols' capitulation after landing in Kyushu in 1274 or 1281.)

In order to have the right to hunt, it was necessary to receive the permission of the local suzerain and to complete various rituals. In particular, the fingers of the applicant were coated with the animal's fat and flesh (the rite of *yaghlamichi*). Kublai and his brother Hülegü killed their first game and were initiated by Genghis Khan when they were eleven and nine years old, respectively. They remained great hunters.

Left: Game reserves, like the *paradesion* of the ancient Iranians—from which the word "paradise" is derived—were created alongside the imperial palaces of Peking. Thus, the Grand Khan did not need to leave the surroundings of the palace to surrender to the pleasures of the hunt. Other parks were situated in various locations throughout the empire, each one specializing in a given species, which did not impede the princes from taking part in the great expeditions of the winter months.

were tracked down in their hidden fortresses and finally eliminated (1256). In Iraq, Baghdad was taken in February 1258 and the Abbasid caliph executed. Nothing could have had more of an effect and more of a symbolic impact. Eastern Christianity was ecstatic. "It has been five hundred and fifteen years," said the Armenian historian Kirakos, "since this city engulfed the whole world." In the wake of Baghdad's collapse, Syria was then almost completely occupied. But it would only take a year for the Mongols to sustain their first and irreparable defeat in this land.

In Syria the Mongols neighbored the Franks, whom they had not touched. The Crusaders there asked themselves: Should they see the Mongols as the vanquishers of Islam, the men who had destroyed with such facility those against whom they had persevered in vain, this people who counted among themselves many Christians and who seemed well disposed toward their faith? Should they listen to the Armenians? But how could one forget what they had done in Europe just ten years ago? The Crusaders' uncertainty and anguish is understandable. Unfortunately, any suggestion of an alliance between them would be short-lived.

The schism of the empire

The year 1260 marked a turning point. With the death of the Grand Khan Mangu in late 1259, Kublai, who commanded China, did not wait for the meeting of the diet or *khuriltai* and, in a true coup d'état, had himself proclaimed sovereign by his troops. Soon after, his younger brother Arigböge did the same in Mongolia. An inexorable schism in the empire developed. War was inevitable between the two sovereigns, and one could see a return to a time when Mongols divided into tribes, each thinking more of their own interests than of the general good. The empire ruptured. After several successes Arigböge finally surrendered in 1264 to his brother, which could have ended the conflict. Instead it fanned the flames. Another prince, Qaidu, a grandson of Ögödei, claimed in his turn the supreme authority of Grand Khan and led in his rebellion the descendants of another son of Genghis Khan, Chagatai, who had had the monopoly in central Asia many years before. A long battle ensued. No longer could one speak of the Mongol Empire except as a symbol. Now there were multiple empires with which to contend. Once the Ögödeid dynasty disappeared, there would be four khanates: one in China that claimed supreme authority and maintained it at least in theory; one in Iran (the Il-khans)—both were heirs of Tolui; the House of Chagatai, descendants of Genghis Khan's second son; and Russia, the Golden Horde or the Kipchak khanate,

Below: "He is a man of good stature, neither short nor tall but of moderate height. His limbs are well fleshed out and modelled in due proportion. His complexion is fair and ruddy like a rose, the eyes black and handsome, the nose shapely and set squarely in place."
Marco Polo, describing Kublai Khan, in *The Travels*

Genghis Khan once said of his grandson Kublai: "Pay attention to the words of this young one. He will succeed me one day and it seems that through him I shall continue to live."

representing the oldest branch, that of Jöchi.

Kublai, the new Grand Khan, appeared readily like a Chinese emperor and could essentially add the name of his Yüan dynasty to the long list of official Chinese dynasties. He acted as one when he transferred the capital of the empire from his grandfather's city, Karakorum in Mongolia, to a place he named the "city of Khan"—Khanbalik (Cambuluc)—or Peking. He remained, however, Grand Khan and a Mongol. If he was

helped by the administration put in place by the Sung, if he named Chinese generals to command his troops—many of whom were Chinese—he also called upon non-Chinese. His guard consisted of thirty thousand Christian Alans (or Alani) from the Caucasus. Armenians lived in his court. He had Iranians as key ministers, like the Muslim Sayyid Ajall of Bukhara, Syrians like Isa (Ai-sie), the Uighur Sanga, and the Tibetan scholar monk Phags-pa (1239–1280), who was at complete liberty to initiate the Mongols into Buddhism.

When it rains, it pours

The same year of 1260, which saw the schism of the empire, also brought the first great defeat. Hülegü had left behind in Syria a very small military contingent under the command of general Kitbuqa, while the majority of the Mongol forces recuperated on the high Iranian plateaus. Everything seemed tranquil. Only one power capable of opposing them remained in this part of the world: Egypt. They were separated by deserts, and Egypt could only have access to Syria by passing through the territories of her enemies, the Crusaders. Egypt was now ruled (1250) by a new regime led by rebellious mercenary

Turks, the Mamluks, and their haughtiness was increased by a stunning victory against Saint Louis (French king Louis IX) in Damietta, Egypt. They had the audacity to demand of the Franks to let them cross their territories. And the Franks, blindly, were foolish enough to accept. The Mamluks surprised the forces of Kitbuqa at Ain Jalut on September 3, 1260, and destroyed them without difficulty. For the first time, the Mongols were chased by an army out of their own territory; for the first time they were defeated on the field of battle. They abandoned Syria. In vain they would try to retake it, most notably in 1299 in the course of a brilliant campaign (the capture of Damascus), but the efforts ultimately would not succeed and rendered futile the intervention of the Chagataid forces. By the end of this century the Mongol khanates had developed the unfortunate habit of making war.

Opposite: The young Tibetan monk Phags-pa met Kublai Khan at a 1258 gathering in Changzhou and established with him the relationship of a donor to a chaplain. Below: Shortly after, the Mongols of Iran tried to establish closer ties to the Franks so that they would join them in battle against the Egyptian Mamluks, who had kept them in check. But the Mongols would be expelled from Syria for the second time after the battle of Homs in 1281.

That a small nomadic people were able to vanquish the great Eurasian powers thanks to their military qualities is stupefying, but even more so is that they knew how to organize their conquests and assure dominance of these highly developed lands. They rallied the common people and the elite, had a talent for administration, and imposed peace and order. Their standard of justice was the same for everyone. They were remarkably tolerant in religious matters and significantly boosted commerce.

CHAPTER 3
HOW THE EMPIRE WAS FOUNDED, HOW THE EMPIRE ENDURED

Two complementary aspects of Mongol life: the invincible cavaliers who would turn to shoot over their shoulders (opposite) and the caravansaries established on the commercial routes of the Near East (right).

Not many...

How many Mongol speakers did Genghis Khan unite
from a nomadic state to conquer the world? There
were not more than some several hundred thousand
individuals and later, when a unified Mongolia
drew together the Naiman, the Tatars, and the Öngüt,
among others, there could not have been a population
of more than a million or a million and a half. What
about the strength of their army, which is often
ignored? At the time of Genghis Khan's death the army
amounted to 129,000 men, not counting some tens of
thousands more who operated in China. This suggests
that one person in ten was enlisted in the army, a
proportion rarely attained by any country and never
for such a long period. To this number, which consti-
tutes the core of the forces, one must add those who
were conscripted one way or another through the course
of the conquests. These individuals formed an incalcu-
lable mass estimated in the hundreds of thousands, if
not in the millions. They say that Genghis Khan promoted three out of ten men in those provinces of which
he made himself the master. And it appears that these
recruits, who initially must have thought only of fleeing,
proved to be faithful, with rare exceptions. Was it fear
of punishment that struck at their weakness or was it
the prestige of the Great Army and the pride of
belonging to it?

All the chroniclers
were struck by the
Mongols' capacity to
withstand a wide variety
of climates and to eat
anything. Above: This
miniature shows Mongols
in the process of drinking
filtered muddy water.
The texts were no less
vivid. Carpini wrote,
"Their food consists of
anything they can put in
their mouths." Marco
Polo said, "When neces-
sary they sit astride their
horses for ten days with-
out any cooked meat
and without making a
fire.... They often do
without wine and water,
living only on the blood
of their horses." As
for Rubruck, he told
Louis IX, "If your
peasants...would
content themselves with
the food [of the Tatar
kings], they could
conquer the whole
world."

Being shackled in a stockade was part of the treatment inflicted on prisoners (below, a 16th-century painting). In his youth Genghis Khan fell into the hands of his enemies and was forced to wear a heavy wooden object that locked together his neck and forearms. The Mongols preferred to use their captives as auxiliaries, laborers, or human shields in their campaigns.

...but invincible

The Mongols compensated for their numerical weakness with the force of their personality. They were a rare type of men. They were endowed with physical vigor and an exceptional morale. They were the survivors of a pitiless natural selection due to the rigors of the climate and the precarious conditions of life. They could endure famine and fatigue just as they supported excesses such as drunkenness and licentiousness. They obeyed blindly. They had a sense of order and of discipline, even more than monks, said Carpini. They would never admit defeat. They fought for their leaders, whom they venerated, and they knew how to protect their lives. Most of all they fought for the pleasure of it—not for the pay but for the glory—and to promote a universal monarchy that would bring peace on earth. They formed a people on the march where the women often fought side by side with men.

In the beginning the Mongols had very little and, to Western eyes, they resembled beggars. They pillaged with abundance, but they shared the spoils and were not seen leaving the battle to devote themselves to

the plunder. In fact, profit did not interest them. They remained attached to their simple lives, and their sole ambition—after taking over the world—was to return to their yurts and their flocks. One of the Mongol's greatest generals, Subotai, who had been governor of the provinces, finished his life living modestly in his childhood tent.

The *tumen*, the bow, and the horse

The army was organized into units of ten: one hundred, one thousand, and ten thousand men, the *tumen*, or divisions, following an ancient custom that goes back to the Achaemenid Persians. To the idea of the traditional solidarity of the clan—a collective soul more powerful than an individual soul—Genghis Khan substituted that of the fighting unit. Each soldier was responsible for all the soldiers in his group. When one failed, all were punished.

They had at their disposal incomparable weapons, the recurved composite bow and the horse, and very quickly learned to make use of unfamiliar objects like cuirasses and siege machines. Starting in 1217 Genghis Khan formed a corps of Chinese artillerymen to wipe out cities, and gunpowder, contrary to popular belief, was used not just for fireworks. The bow, light for shooting near, heavy for shooting far, was more effective than anything else. (However it was no match for the crossbow, which is eventually why there were Frankish crossbowmen in the Mongol army.) The horse of the steppes, a "double" pony, was small, stocky, vigorous, sturdy, quick, and capable of feeding itself on even the meagerest of pastures. It could dig out grass from under a blanket of snow, run across the rocks like a goat, and race up to 60 miles (100 kilometers) a day when it was well fed and well rested, which is why the Mongols preferred winter campaigns when the horses were stuffed full of summer grass. Each

Below: This engraving illustrates the text of an 18th-century traveler and describes the structure of a yurt (lattice, arch, felt, and calotte at the apex) as well as its interior organization. Particularly notable are the hearth placed in the center of the space and the domestic idols (*ongons*)—dolls made of felt or wood—posed on the ground.

For the Mongol, the horse was indispensable. He lived on it. He drew from it his favorite drink, koumiss, the fermented mare's milk that contained 5% alcohol. From the foals' manes cut in the spring, he made tethers and rope. Sometimes he drank the horse's blood by pressing his mouth to an open vein. Opposite and left: A Mongol accorded his horse all his care, and the veterinary works concerning horses were plentiful. He began to break in a horse when it was two years old. He gelded it when it was in its third year, keeping whole only those males needed for reproduction. He tied up or braided its mane and very thick tail. He shoed the horse regularly, and with a red-hot iron branded it with the mark of a seal, the *tamga*, a sign of ownership as well as a religious symbol. Its theft was considered one of the worst crimes that could be committed and was severely punished. The horse served him and he loved it, and it was not contradictory to put one to death in order to inter with its master.

man who went to combat possessed at least three horses in order always to have a fresh mount and, according to some, that number could be five or six times higher. The Mongol was at one with the horse, used as he was to riding him from the earliest age. He lived with it, ate with it, and slept by it, and no horseman could ever be his equal.

A perfect tactic

War, contrary to the simplistic image that often accompanies it, was neither a torrent of unorganized hordes nor a quick operation. Every campaign was prepared with care and carried out with thought and meticulousness. Scouts were sent to check out trails. Depots of supplies were positioned in prearranged spots. Water outlets were controlled. The Mongol generals were master tacticians and often military geniuses who improvised when it was necessary but who preferred to stick to their plans. In general they did not expose their positions but kept at a distance in order to overlook the operations and not risk their lives, not for fear of death but because they knew that their deaths would generate panic. They avoided great battles, preferring harassment, which exhausted and demoralized the enemy. When the Mongols encountered an army that was too strong for them, they feigned flight in order to lead them into pursuit, knowing that the tactic would put the enemy in disarray. This way they could choose the place where they intended to fight, leading the opposing troops into a trap, and then the Mongol warriors would do an about-face when it was least expected. The mounted archers would then turn around and shoot over their shoulders. If they had to abandon the battle, they would occupy the surrounding heights and put the weakest elements, such as the foreign recruits, in the center—a mass of bodies who could absorb the first attack—while the flanks, formed of the elite, carried out a vast encircling maneuver.

All ruses were acceptable when it came to fooling the enemy. They pitched fake bivouacs and lit campfires where there were no camps. They dressed straw mannequins as soldiers and used prisoners as human ramparts.

After having been in contact with sedentary cultures, the Mongols quickly learned new techniques from them, particularly military techniques. These proved indispensable for seizing cities that otherwise had to be tricked or starved out. Above, on the Tigris in Baghdad: They learned to use bridges made of boats for crossing the largest rivers.

They charged with frightening cries like *"Ur ah!"* most likely from which the word "hurrah" is derived. The effectiveness of this propaganda was astonishing. Even far from the front, there were the most terrifying and outrageous noises. The medieval chroniclers echoed these cries and contributed in great measure to discouraging the adversary, if the cities in ruins and the massacres had not already done so. All this devastation was not carried out simply to spread terror but to show what awaited those who preferred to resist rather than to yield.

A well-administered empire

The qualities that served the Mongols in war also served them in peace, but it was necessary to have others as well. As Ögödei said: "The empire was created on horseback but it cannot be governed on horseback." Even though they increased their decrees—in 1225 Rashid ad-Din witnessed the multiplicity of imperial ordinances—the Mongols knew that they did not have enough administrative experience. They put out a call to foreigners for help and left behind them the commissars, the *darugatchi*, to watch over them.

Uighurs and Khitans became their first bureaucrats and, later, Iranians, Chinese, and Syrians were added to their ranks. In the spring of 1220 Genghis Khan had already begun the restoration of Sogdiana by putting into place offices charged with maintaining records in Persian and in Uighur, establishing a census of the inhabitants, levying taxes, and recruiting soldiers and

From the earliest antiquity, nomads knew how to build. The Hsiung-nu (Huns) are credited with the defensive system established in the north of Mongolia used to protect themselves against attacks from the Siberians, and there are vestiges of Turkic funerary temples from the 6th to 8th centuries. Below: Lookout towers raised by the Genghis-khanites in high places allowed the Mongols not just to survey the land but to transmit visible messages far away with the aid of fires, which they would light on the summit.

workers. And there were plenty who joined the
Mongols. Although it sometimes cost them
dearly since they were serving the conquerors and
collaborating with the occupiers, in doing so
these people saved their countries. They had a
premonition without a doubt. Two men in
particular sped up eastern Iran's recovery: Mas'ud
and Mahmud Yalavach, a father and son who were
appointed by the Mongols as financial administrators around 1221, and for life. Mahmud was even
called on to end his days as governor of Peking (from
1240–1254). Later on a Chinese source shows Ögödei
occupied with taking a census so that he could hire
the educated inhabitants and give them administrative duties in their hometowns.

Peace and quiet

What may have played the biggest role in favor of the
Mongols despite internal or foreign wars, conclusively
marginal, was the establishment of peace and order.
Finished were the tribal conflicts, finished was the fighting
between small states and their neighbors, eliminated
without pity were troublemakers, bandits who plagued
the main roads, religious fanatics, persecutors of the
weak, and sects like the Ismailians of Iran who perpetrated political crimes. As long as the empire was strong,
it was possible—even if the distance and the nature of
the terrain remained great obstacles—to cross Eurasia
from the Mediterranean or the Black Sea to the Pacific.

For that reason alone the Mongol peace would have
been enough to encourage travels and commerce, but the
government's interest in the paths of communication and
negotiations fostered it even more. From 1220 to 1221
Genghis Khan opened routes in previously inaccessible
territories in Afghanistan and Khorasan. It was a matter
of reaching the rebels. But the emperor understood the
interest in linking up the diverse provinces, not by
the paths paved in Roman times, although there were
still some in China, but by reliable, unobstructed trails
equipped with rest stops, watering holes, and food supplies, with workhorses and guarded by soldiers. In the

Above: Chinese bank
notes seemed such a
marvel to the Westerners
but the form of currency
did not prove to be pop-
ular in the west of the
empire. (Introduced in
Iran in 1294, it provoked
riots.) The bills carried
the seal of the sovereign,
which alone authenticated
them, and each counter-
feit was punishable by
death "up to the third
generation."

quriltai of 1235 Ögödei decided to establish a network of rest stops (*djam* or *yam*) between Mongolia and the provinces that were, in principle, reserved for the imperial couriers. For the slow-moving caravans, he gave functionaries the responsibility of digging wells. He abolished taxes that hurt the merchants, with the exception of those on luxury goods. In China the ancient routes were restored, planted with trees, and equipped with inns, and the Grand Canal that connected Peking and Hangzhou was entirely redeveloped. Thus the empire experienced intense trading and banking activities, and the influx of riches generated a cultural flowering that was, to say the least, unexpected after the devastation of war.

Left: The imperial seal written in Mongol characters borrowed from the Uighurs changed somewhat over the years, but the text varied little: "With the force of the eternal Heaven, by the order of the universal Grand Khan of the Mongol people. If he comes to submissive people they will respect him and they will fear him."

Paper money (*ch'ao*) did not eliminate pieces of silver or gold nor the payments in silk that had been accepted since antiquity. Below: Accounts were carefully noted in writing. The payment of taxes that the Grand Khan levied on commercial products was rendered heavier by the devaluation of 1282.

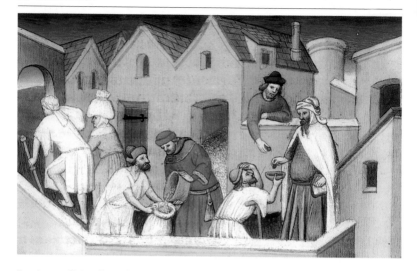

Justice, solicitude, tolerance, and an absence of racism

The attention to administration allowed the empire to flourish, even though some of the administrators did not always prove themselves to be up to their tasks. Of course some dreamed of enriching themselves, and their misappropriation of public funds and their dishonesty astonished the Mongols, who were themselves incorruptible. They clamped down. Their justice was implacable but it was the same for everyone. Even the most grand did not escape it. Güyük did not hesitate to execute the all-powerful minister Abd ar-Rahman because he exploited the Chinese people, and Rashid ad-Din (1247–1318), who was the vizier for the Il-khans in Iran for twenty years, ended up under the executioner's blade.

This equality before the law was appreciated, as was the concern for the most impoverished. There was an absence of racism, and in general there existed a universal tolerance, despite the fanatics who readily refused to others the rights they themselves were accorded.

Solicitude? Kublai made arrangements in 1260 to provide for aged scholars, for orphans, and for the sick.

In order to maintain the royal courts, to cope with years of famine, and to help the destitute (above, a Western vision offered by Marco Polo), the Chinese state bought agricultural surpluses and stored them in closely guarded public granaries. This kind of attention to the poor may appear to be a Buddhist influence, but its origin is more likely found in the various social organisms, such as hospices, that had long existed in Muslim countries.

In 1271 he ordered the creation of hospices. In each city he organized the distribution of foodstuffs for the needy. Marco Polo related that the *Qaghan* himself fed thirty thousand indigents daily.

Tolerance? Innumerable edicts were promulgated in favor of diverse religious communities throughout the empire. Interdenominational conferences were organized by princes, Buddhism spread in Confucian and Taoist countries, Christianity was everywhere, and the erection of numerous pagodas and churches in Muslim countries bears witness to the Mongol attitude of openness.

Absence of racism? The Mongols certainly created Mongolism but there is no trace of exaltation of the race. The only exaltation, and one that endured, was for Genghis Khan. Far from assimilating the vanquished, the Mongols ended up largely Turkified, like in the Golden Horde and in the khanate of Chagatai. And nowhere did they, like the Romans, Arabs, Turks, or English, impose their own language.

Of all the alleged conversions by Mongol princes to Christianity, that of the Grand Khan Mangu, announced by the Armenian historian Hayton, was the one that caused the greatest stir. His baptism, represented above, is a myth. But the sovereign was the son of a Christian woman, had the Kereyid Nestorian Christian Bolghai as an advisor, and treated Christians very well. Muslims maintained on their part that he had become a Muslim, and Buddhists saw in him a fellow believer. Their declarations only prove that he did not adopt any of the great universal religions, but that he sought to make them live in peace and in harmony.

In the Mongol Empire Christians benefited from the enviable position that their alliance with the Armenian monarchy brought them in the Near East. Opposite: That ancient culture—here evoked by the celebrated 10th-century church of Aghtamar situated in an islet in Lake Van, Turkey—exercised a great influence, although perhaps only on Romanesque art. Muslims complained that under the domination of the Il-khans, a new church was constructed every day. Mosques were also built, but Islam was never well accepted by the Chinese, despite the amount of Sinicizing it submitted itself to in order to be established with them. This page, top: This undated mosque in Xiahe in eastern China could easily be mistaken for a pagoda. Bottom: But those monuments that escaped the destruction engendered by assaults, like the 10th-century mausoleum of Ismail the Samanid in Bukhara, were well maintained and would begin again to exercise their influence on an Islamic architecture in full rebirth.

The century of Mongol domination was one not only of great scientific and artistic fulfillment but also of a profound renewal of inspiration due to the emergence of popular traditions long suppressed by scholars and the elite, the promotion of the lower social classes, and the influences that diverse civilizations exercised on each other.

CHAPTER 4
A WORLD OF WONDER AND SURPRISE

Opposite: The tomb of Öljeitü in Solta-niyeh, his Iranian capital, shows the fidelity of the nomads to the traditions of the steppes, and the breach of Koranic laws that banned funerary art. Right: Similarly, the figure of a prince seated cross-legged on an early-14th-century vase departs from traditional repre-sentations of sovereigns on thrones.

The renewal of arts and sciences

The empire was immensely rich and had the means to be the patron of the arts; like the state, many private individuals had money and an interest in culture. The conquerors had not carefully spared the lives of so many artisans during the plunder of cities only to let them sit idle, and so the artisans continued to work even as the fighting continued. While many buildings were crumbling, astonishingly, there was also much construction of new ones, like the mausoleum of Imam Yahya, erected around 1260 in Varamin, south of Tehran. Even more remarkable was the creation and the flowering of the great observatory of Maragha (1259), a scientific institution that represented one of the highest achievements of world astronomy and that was embodied by the great philosopher and mathematician Nasir ad-Din Tusi (1201–1274).

A bove: This drawing of the planetary movements is of a sophisticated culture. Below: A terra-cotta statue representing a Chinese actor demonstrates the growth of popular culture.

China borrowed from Iran the art of cloisonné enamels, like the inlay of precious metals in lacquer, as well as new ceramic techniques, such as the cobalt-blue–glazed porcelain and the famous blue-and-white family of porcelain, which would remain popular throughout the centuries. From the middle of the 13th century they borrowed the weaving of carpets from the nomads, who to date had had the exclusive monopoly, and they made a great success of it. The promotion of the common people and the Mongol taste for popular art, notably for the theater that was so denigrated by the Jin and the Sung, allowed this art form to acquire letters of patent—that is, a formal grant from the conquerors. This support led to the origin of a new poetic genre in China, *san-kuo*, a theatrical and literary form that was based on vernacular language and everyday life.

Iran was also the birthplace of the "modern" school of history, led by the genius of the vizier Rashid ad-Din, founder of the great library of Tabriz. His *Jami al-*

Tawarikh (*World History*) was not just a history but something greater—explanatory, conceptual, and global in its scope. In the Near East the influence of China, which had been apparent since the Seljuk era, became even more evident, especially in the work of ceramists, weavers, and painters.

In those lands with less grand traditions, like the region of the Golden Horde, archaeological excavations of cities founded by the Mongols have revealed quantities of objects, particularly in metal that attest to the high mastery of their artisans.

Astronomy was an ancient science in Muslim countries but, before the 8th century, it was the occupation of isolated researchers. The observatory of Maragha, where excavations have provided an understanding of the ground and elevation plans, was the first great establishment dedicated to the study of the heavens. There, built around the teachings of the master Nasir ad-Din Tusi, a number of scholars unified their efforts in a collective work. New instruments were invented, celestial maps abounded, knowledge took great leaps forward. The *Il-khanides Tables* (*Zij-i Il-khani*), written in Persian and translated into Arabic, had a vast audience that would eventually be lost. Left: This Persian manuscript illustrates that in the 15th century Tusi was still presented teaching in his observatory, even though his supposed students— old men with white beards—were most likely his colleagues. The influence of Maragha and Tusi is linked across two centuries to the observatory of the learned Timurid sovereign Ulugh Beg at Samarkand, whose scientific works were still considered authoritative in the 19th century.

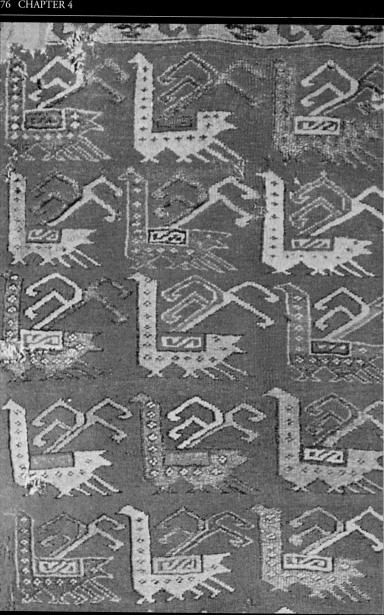

Opposite: The texts of antiquity included references to carpets (maybe thick fabrics), but carpets were the privilege of the nomads who spread them throughout the world. Their existence dates from at least the 2nd or 3rd century BC from examples found in Pazyryk in the Altai, and there are also fragments from the 3rd to 4th centuries AD discovered in Xinjiang. The Seljuks introduced carpets to Iran and Anatolia—where many 13th-century specimens with their dominant tones of blue and soft reds have been discovered—and the Mongols brought them to China.

The close ties between Iranian and Chinese art are apparent in these two roughly contemporary plates (8th–9th centuries AD). This page, top: The Persian-style plate called *minai* depicts a horseman and his falcon. The rider has a very Mongol face, "in the shape of the moon," which was the ideal of beauty at that time. Bottom: This dragon plate was made in the China of the Yüans. The blue-and-white style captivated China for a long time but would not be forgotten in Muslim countries where beautiful works were still produced in the 18th century.

Although they submitted to the influence of the settled civilizations, the nomads continued the art of the steppes. Like the Scythians long before them, they used precious metals to fashion utilitarian objects and, particularly, religious or princely ones such as this ceremonial saddle decorated in silver (opposite) and the golden cup (this page, top) used to offer libations to the gods and the earth. Both works date from the 8th century and come from Mongolia and the Golden Horde, respectively. Although the great workshops of China and Iran suffered from the invasions and sometimes disappeared completely, their production reemerged soon after in a new approach that melded diverse traditions. The Seljuk ceramics of Iran were revived in the Sultanabad style, which produced original, often Sinicized works at the beginning of the 14th century. Middle and bottom: The fragile glaze of this series of bowls with flared walls on a small base makes it difficult to judge the lovely effect of the gray-blue or beige design.

The School of Tabriz

It may not be a coincidence that in the Near East, as in China, art found its greatest means of expression in painting. Even though some artists in China steered clear of the new ruling power, many placed themselves in its service. Landscapes, painted on vertical scrolls in a centuries-old and unchanged technique, were still preferred, but new subjects also appeared: scenes of hunting and of war, horses, and portraits. Masters abounded, among them Li-k'an, Chao Meng-fu (1254–1322), called Tzu-ang, and his wife, Khauan Tao-Chang, painter of bamboo and orchids, Tchou-To, and with them a galaxy of artists. Painters of the "Arab" school from Baghdad, which had been destroyed by Mongols, had taken refuge in Tabriz, capital of the Il-khans, and created there the birthplace of the classical Persian miniature. The horizontal plane was abandoned for the vertical one—the page. Compositions were now enclosed within a frame but borders were often broken by illustrations. Action was situated in a natural environment where the sky was pushed back to the very top of the image, and a different sort of perspective was invented by the superimposition of characters on various levels without the use of perspective. New decorative elements appeared, all of a Far Eastern origin, such as gnarled trees, clouds in the forms of Chinese dragons, and mountainous peaks.

Regarding painting, reciprocal influences between China and Iran are evident in the Mongol era, but China's great artisans also knew how to resist the lessons of the conquerors. Although it evolved and developed a new approach that would become known as the Ming style, Chinese painting maintained a spare aesthetic that brought out the internal power of the work. Above: This monochrome landscape, in which the pavilion barely appears, contrasts a tree with its twisted branches against the emptiness of the background that accentuates the purity of the work and its spiritual density.

The concerns of architecture

Despite the previous manifestations of the art, it was during the reigns of Ghazan and Öljeitü that architecture reached its peak. Compared to the worthy and often beautiful structures, like the Imamzade Zafer (1326) and the mausoleum of Baba Kasem (1340) in Isfahan, or the

Great Mosque in Natanz (1324), or the tomb of the Persian mystic Imam Safi ad-Din (1334) in Ardebil, the new rulers created two great masterpieces: the tomb of Öljeitü in Soltaniyeh (1316), a prototype for the mausoleums that would become typical in Islam, notably in India; and the *mihrab*, which bore the name of Öljeitü, in the Great Mosque of Isfahan, whose decorative finesse contrasts with the weightiness of the citadel of Tabriz (1324).

Architecture flourished even in the peripheral provinces controlled by the Mongols, with examples like

Left: This Iranian minia-ture of the Mongol era belatedly illustrates a subject extremely popular in the Muslim world and about which illustrated manuscripts abounded: the fables of the Indian Bidpai. Composed in Sanskrit c. 300 BC, the *Panchatranta* were translated into Arabic by Ibn al-Muqaffa in the 8th century and into classical Iranian Pahlavi, or literary Persian, later. Its heroes are two treach-erous and unscrupulous jackals, Kalila and Dimna, who would meet a tragic end. Their innumerable adventures were a pretext for moralistic tales aimed at the great and the pow-erful of the world. The spirit in which the page is treated is rather Sinicized, with a somewhat spare composition, large rocks formed like waves in the foreground, dragon-shape clouds in a starry sky, and a very promi-nent tree—less "tortured" than a typical Chinese depiction but still with an Eastern echo about it. These Asian conventions contrast with a kind of poetic Muslim idealism and almost a realism in the treatment of the painting's animals and the reproduction of the flowers.

Opposite, bottom: Late-12th-century minaret of Jam in Afghanistan. Color was applied in certain areas of the exterior surface of Muslim monuments by using blocks of enameled bricks composing epigraphic friezes, which would have been invisible and unreadable without it. Color continued to gain ground and finally covered most of the exterior surface. Opposite, top: The Blue Mosque of Tabriz, capital of the Mongols in Iran since Ghazan (1293), offers a perfect example of color application. Page 85: Although its exterior is now very dilapidated, the Blue Mosque was rebuilt by the Timurids in the 15th century. Left: Sheik Abu Yazid (Bayazid) al-Bistami was one of the first mystics to advocate the doctrine of annihilation by God (*fena*). The existing version of his tomb in Bistam, in Iran, with its monumental porch and the conical roof of the mausoleum, dates primarily from the period of Ghazan and Öldjeitü, but the minaret, a beautiful achievement of the Seljuk era, was constructed somewhat earlier, around 1120.

Even though they are roughly contemporary, the two ceramic techniques represented here are quite different. Left: The Blue Mosque of Tabriz is covered primarily in a floral decoration, like the interlacing design of an arabesque whose demi-palmettes each give birth to a new flowering stem. Opposite: This great composition, which comes from Kashan, Iran, and is now held by the Louvre in Paris, is made of a pattern of crosses and stars fitted one into the other and set off with thick bands of framing. The flora is somewhat naturalistic, but the abundance of real and imaginary creatures (such as the dragon in the blue star below) are full of verve and life—although the human heads are haloed and the bodies positioned somewhat stiffly. In the bottom left-hand corner, one notes the often-reproduced image of a lion overlapping the sun, which would become the coat of arms of the Iranian monarchy.

the Timur Hane (hospital) in Amasia in eastern Anatolia or the Yakutiye *madrasa* (Islamic teaching college) in Erzurum, Turkey, both from 1308.

These nomads, who so often detested cities, were now attentive to architecture and were not content with embellishing already existing towns. They created new ones, sometimes out on the open steppes, like the city of Djötchi in southern Siberia, Shangdu in the southern Gobi, the two Sarai of Batu and Berke in the Golden Horde, Astrakhan, Fergana, and Andizhan. And they filled these cities with people. Under Mongol domination, the urban population increased inordinately. It was staggering to Westerners for whom Paris, then Europe's largest city, did not exceed two hundred thousand souls. They spoke of the million inhabitants of Tabriz, of the eight million in Hangzhou. Perhaps they exaggerated.

A fabulous world

The Mongol Empire, and the Far East above all, possessed everything that could seduce a Westerner. However, it was neither art nor nature that interested them. It was people and their achievements. They were enchanted by the people who made the cities and lived in them. When cities no longer carried traces of devastation—which was still perceptible here and there in places like Bactra

Two reliefs placed face-to-face (above, one of the two), from the Yakutiye *madrasa* in Erzurum, illustrate the myths and cosmogenic visions of the people of the steppes. At the top of the great tree of life, the bearer of fruits and birds and supported by two lions confronting each other, sits an eagle, the messenger of the heavens. A solar, or more likely lunar, globe dominates the scene.

(Balkh)—visitors were dazzled. Samarkand, for example, was said to be one of the greatest and most beautiful cities of the world. But many felt nothing could equal the splendor of China. Before they knew the country, travelers imagined there would be "ribbons of silver walls and ramparts of gold," and they were seldom disappointed by the infinite supply of marvelous, stunning, and unimaginable things.

The European traveler discovered, first of all, an expanse of territory that he had never suspected. He often had no inkling about Chinese ways of comportment, thinking, believing, or living; of techniques and sciences; of

Above: An annex room to the Great Mosque of Isfahan houses the stucco *mihrab* of Öljeitü (the empty niche indicates the direction of Mecca). The remarkable lacework speaks to a rarely attained architectural finesse and elegance, while the somewhat pervasive epigraphy plays against the charming floral motifs.

housing, dress, or food and drink; of plants and animals. He didn't know if what he saw was real or if he was a victim of his imagination or some diabolical manifestation and, finally, he had no choice but to accept it. Returning home he wrote his memoirs, and with the same pen he described things he had seen and things that had been told to him. Why are fairy tales less credible than these fabulous observations? It's not just the monsters that surprised the writer; he often spoke of them and they filled his imagination for many years. No,

Below: The central Asian painter Mehmet Siyah Kalem created a fantasy world peopled by beings showing a brutal realism, very different from the fabulous jinn and roc birds that populate the imaginary worlds of Islam.

the foreign observer could accept men with heads of dogs, those without heads, those who didn't speak, were hairy, carried themselves bent over (Were these the great apes?), hermaphrodites, dwarfs, and giants. What was most surprising to him is no longer surprising today: the dogma of reincarnation, shamanic seances, conjurers' towers, the scholars' inordinately long nails, the tiny bound feet of Chinese women, dogs that led carts without wheels, lands where the sun never rose or never set, money made of salt, shells, or pieces of paper, burning stones that emitted a powerful heat, the elephants or unicorns (which could only be rhinoceroses).

"As they traversed the deserts they found there other monsters in human form. They had but a hand in the middle of their stomachs and only one foot...and they ran so quickly that the fastest horse could not keep up with them."
Giovanni da Pian del Carpini from *History of the Mongols*

A remarkable liberalism

The Mongol Empire prompted a cross-fertilization of peoples without precedent in history before our contemporary era. Turks, Mongols, Iranians, and Chinese went to Europe. Their thoughts remain only in the fragments of text sent by Rabban Bar Sauma. Refugees brought with them the cultures that had formed them. Jalal ad-Din ar-Rumi (1207–1273), born in Bactra, emigrated to Konya, Turkey, where he founded an order of whirling dervishes and renewed Muslim mysticism in the Near East with its powerful and original Bactrian roots. The Persian poet Amir Khusraw (d. 1325), who emigrated to India, strengthened Iranian culture there.

Europeans who went to Asia found themselves brutally confronted by the Nestorians, whose vision of Christianity was neither Catholic nor Orthodox, by Buddhist "idolators," with whom they clashed, and by Muslims, whom they saw simply as heretics.

This page: Like the unicorn, dog-headed men had been sighted all over Asia and everyone talked about them, perhaps because the name *noqai*, "dog," was one of the more common in the Mongol era. The Armenian Hayton spoke of one country "where the women are reasonable in the manner of men and the men are without reason and resemble dogs." Marco Polo wrote, "Know that the men of this island all have heads of dogs and teeth and eyes like dogs."

Of prisoners, volunteers, ambassadors, and merchants

There were countless prisoners, like those Germans whom the missionaries sought in vain, installed in Talas (now Zhambyl) and then in Dzungaria (now Junggar) as miners and makers of arms; a small colony of French captured in Belgrade, whom Rubruck met in Mongolia; and the Parisian goldsmith Guillaume Buchier whom he found in Karakorum, and the woman from Metz, France, named Paquette, whose husband was an architect for Mangu.

The doctrine of Nestorius, which taught that the human and divine natures of Christ were separate (and therefore refused to recognize Mary as the mother of God), was condemned at the Council of Ephesus in 431 AD. It spread in Asia, however, where it gave birth to an independent church under the authority of a patriarch first installed in Seleucia and then in Baghdad. Solidly planted in Iran, Nestorianism also played a great role in the genesis of Islamic science with the medical school of Djundichapur, and when it won over Sogdiana, Serindia—where it was called "dominant" by the Uighurs—and China, where its monasteries were designated "from Persia." Left: A 15th-century illustration from central Asia. The religion flourished in the Mongol era. A Turko-Öngüt from the Far East named Mar Yaballaha III had the good fortune to be elected patriarch in 1281 and played a major role in the life of the khanate of Iran. When the county turned to Islam, the patriarch was arrested in 1295, tortured, and then set free, but he remained out of favor for the rest of his life, presaging the irremediable decline of his church.

Hungarians and Russians were found everywhere, and descendants of the Muslims who introduced Islam to Yün-nan still exist there today. There were those who went voluntarily and those who were sent. There were so many of them that it is easy to forget the efforts they made to accomplish the journey, the ordeals they surmounted, and that many among them lost their lives. It may seem short by modern standards, but the journey from western Europe to the Far East at that time was long, whether by the maritime route or over land. By sea it took, in principle, about eight months to sail from Egypt or the Persian Gulf to the ports of China, but in reality one could wander for two years or more. By the overland route, Florentine merchant Francesco Balducci Pegolotti estimated it was necessary to count 265 days from Crimea to the Chinese Grand Canal. His estimation seems accurate. Diplomatic voyagers (not the imperial post) took five to seven months to traverse Asia, if everything went well; merchants and private individuals were even slower.

There were thousands of ambassadors like the ones Benoit of Poland and Carpini saw in Güyük's court. Georgians, Arabs, Koreans, Chinese, and Indians were there, and many others followed. There were adventurers who entered the Mongols' service or came to try their chance with them, and Italian merchants were well installed in Tabriz and in the Golden Horde, where they battled in fierce competition for business; and present in India, China, and elsewhere were Pisans, Florentines, Venetians, and above all Genovese, according to Pegolotti, who described their routes and Asiatic stopping places and gave weights and measures in the Genovese system. There are no traces of them in the Celestial Empire before the arrival of the Polo brothers in 1275, but it is doubtful there had not been predecessors. Several names emerge, like that of a young Venetian woman whose tomb was rediscovered in Yangzhou in 1961. They rubbed shoulders with the discreet Jews, who were intensely active in Iran but whose presence in the Far East is perceived

Left: Born in 1182, the Franciscan Giovanni da Pian del Carpini was more than sixty years old when he was chosen to direct one of the first missions sent by the papacy to the Mongols. Leaving Lyons, France, in April 1245, he crossed Poland, the Ukraine, and the Volga River and arrived in Mongolia in July 1246 to assist in the election of Güyük by the *khuriltai*. He returned in the middle of winter and reached Kiev in May 1247. He was the first European to have voluntarily crossed Asia.

Opposite, bottom: In 1253 Saint Louis (King Louis IX) dispatched another Franciscan, William of Rubruck, to the Mongols. Rubruck was an exceptional person, not only courageous like his predecessor Carpini but radiating faith, joy, spirit, energy, and mischief. He departed from Constantinople in May 1253, reached Mongolia six months later, left there in July 1254, and arrived in Cyprus in June 1255. His superior kept him in a monastery there where he had to write a long letter to the king relating his voyage, and thus was born one of the masterpieces of medieval literature, *Travels to the Mongol Empire*.

only by chance in the texts of the time. One mentions an emigration of people from Narbonne, France, which was an important center of the Jews in the Middle Ages, and another the 1365 restoration of a synagogue.

The Muslims were omnipresent and often powerful. The Tibetans, whom Kublai attracted to his court and who preached Tibetan Buddhism there, also went to Iran, where they erected pagodas in Soltaniyeh in Tabriz. In Sarai, in the khanate of Kipchak, the city had Mongol, Russian, Turk, Cherkess, Byzantine, and Arab neighborhoods. They say that in Karakorum, Genghis Khan's capital, one could find twelve temples to idols of various nations, two mosques, and one church. One

The 1375 Catalan atlas of Abraham Cresques is more a compendium of drawings than maps like those created by astronomer Ptolemy in the 2nd century AD or by the cartographer ash-Sharif al-Idrisi in 1154. Above: The collection was illustrated and captioned according to the tales of Marco Polo (and here shows a caravan going to China). The world had to wait for cartographer Mercator, before a real atlas would be published in 1576.

rich Armenian matron built, at her cost, a magnificent church, which was entrusted to Gerard Albuini, bishop of Zayton (now Quanzhou, China).

Catholic aims

Starting in 1260 Catholic missions acted behind the scenes. They were numerous, primarily in Iran, where Jean de Sultaniye (1332) distinguished himself, and in the Kipchak, which Jerome de Catalogne, bishop of Crimea at the beginning of the 14th century, notably frequented. They quickly won over central Asia, India, and the Far East. Giovanni da Montecorvino, sent by Pope Nicholas IV in 1289, was the true founder of Chinese Catholicism. Although he was well received by the imperial authorities, he suffered intrigues at the hands of the Nestorians, who were present everywhere in the empire. The Nestorians were at the root of the Roman church's disappointed but always revitalized expectations concerning the conversion of the Mongols, and they probably also spread the

In 1245 Pope Innocent IV sent two Dominican and two Franciscan missions to the Mongols. Ascelin of Cremona directed the first of the Dominican embassies. Above: Here he is shown receiving the message from the pope destined for General Baidu. From France, he reached his hosts in the Transcaucases in 1247, where he proved to be a terrible diplomat, finding a way to get on the wrong side of even the Christians. Fortunately, he was accompanied by Simon of Saint-Quentin, a good observer, who wrote one of the first accounts of travels to Asia.

legend about Prester Jean, a mysterious Eastern potentate who set back Islam. Montecorvino had numerous subordinates: Andrew of Perugia, who arrived in Peking in 1313; Franciscan friar Odoric of Pordenone (1325); Gerard Albuini; and Franciscan friar Giovanni dei Marignolli, who first visited the Golden Horde around 1340 and then was archbishop of Peking from 1342 to 1346.

The missionaries' tales

The expulsion of the Mongols from China in 1369 put an end to this spectacular adventure, though it lived on in literature. Merchants wrote little, missionaries more. Marco Polo's description of the marvels of the Eastern world is certainly the most famous, but there exist others. The travel narratives of Giovanni da Pian del Carpini, William of Rubruck, French Dominican friar Simon of Saint-Quentin, Hayton of Armenia, Jourdain de Séverac, Jean de Cor, even the gullible Odoric of Pordenone, the first European to have seen Lhasa, are sometimes more precise and more passionate. The well-documented imposter and pseudovoyager Sir John Mandeville, who did not even leave his home, wrote the most successful book of them all. Thanks to these narratives, we have a nuanced view of life in the Mongol Empire. Thanks to them, the great maritime discoveries took place some one hundred and fifty years later.

Hayton—the religious figure not to be confused with the eponymous king of Armenia (also known as Hethum)—became a monk in Cyprus, where he had emigrated in 1305 after having served in the battle against the Egyptian Mamluks. He then went to live in a monastery in Poitiers, France. Shortly before his death, to attract attention from the pope it is said he dictated his memoirs in French to Nicolas Falcon around 1307. Below: His book *La Flore des estoires de la terre d'Orient* (which he presents in this illustration to John the Fearless, Duke of Burgundy) is one of the most interesting medieval accounts of those dedicated to the history of the Mongols. Though its author has

been forgotten, the work still maintains its deservedly important reputation.

There were in fact—if not by right—four independent states (*ulus*) in the Mongol Empire after 1260. Two were destined for a brief but splendid existence. The third, at the end of the 14th century, would give birth to the Timurid empire. The fourth, that of the Kipchak, also called the Golden Horde, would dominate Russia for two hundred and fifty years, and its heirs would still reign at the beginning of the 20th century.

CHAPTER 5

THE FOUR EMPIRES AND THE DECLINE

Opposite: Although the battle of Kulikovo in 1380 was not decisive, it became the symbol of the liberation of Russia, and over the centuries the Russians evoked the memory of it. Here is a detail of a painting from 1680. Right: It is also in memory of Mongol grandeur that Zahir-ud-Din Muhammad (Babur), founder of the Mughal empire, paid homage to his Mongol uncle, Ahmed Khan, in 1502.

A unified and glorious China...on the decline

In the east was the China of the Yüan, a China finally unified, larger than it had ever been or would ever be again. It encompassed Manchuria and Korea, Tibet, part of Xinjiang, and Siberia, and dominated more or less directly over many states of Southeast Asia. Its external politics were aggressive, and its internal politics would be judged severely—and not unjustly—by the Chinese of a subsequent era, who saw in it military dictatorship, oppression, and economic exploitation.

It experienced at least several decades of glory during the reign of Kublai Khan (1260–1294) and that of his first successor and grandson, Oljäi Temür (1294–1307), and even under Khaishan (1307–1311) and Buyantu (1311–1320). But with the death of the latter, the battles over succession brought China into decline. Princes, who would only mount the throne in order to descend it as quickly as possible, were weak, debauched, and senile. The misappropriation of public funds prevailed everywhere, and Buddhism, whose influence was great and highly esteemed—like Christianity—was incapable of curbing the problem. The genuine popular opposition that appeared around 1350 transformed itself into an armed insurrection, then expanded and swept the country. The last Great Khan was expelled in 1369. The deposed Mongols returned with him to live on the steppes.

Above: Ghazan's conversion to Islam (here with his spouse and court) marked a turning point in the history of the Mongols in Iran, even though this prince remained faithful to the national traditions and the lessons of his ancestors. Although fundamentalism was quickly suppressed under his reign, he could not prevent Iran's return to its Islamic nature, which asserted itself under Öljeitü. Mongol domination lost its reason for being and collapsed shortly thereafter.

Iran under Muslim pressure

In Iran it had already been thirty years since the Mongols had been eliminated. After the reigns of Hülegü (1256–1265), Abaqa (1265–1282), and Arghun (1284–1291), Muslim pressure became irresistible under Gaikhatu (1291–1295) and Ghazan (1295–1304), a prince whose brilliant reign would be clouded at the beginning by a short and violent flare-up of fanaticism against Jews, Buddhists, and Christians. The pressure ended by sweeping away everything under the reign of Öljeitü (1304–1316), so much so that Iran reconnected with its past and appeared from then on more like a Muslim state than a Mongol one. When the Öngüt Nestorian patriarch Mar Yaballaha III died in semi-disgrace in 1317, not just a great figure in Mongol history disappeared but an entire epoch went with him. In an unfortunate coincidence, the all-powerful minister Rashid ad-Din, a converted Jew, good politician, and historian of genius even if a somewhat disreputable character, was executed a year later. Under the lazy ruler Abu Sa'id (1317–1336), the society and the state decomposed so much and to such a degree, that when the Il-khan leader died without a direct heir, no one wanted to succeed him. The country sank into complete anarchy.

The three great princes descended from Hülegü, Genghis Khan's grandson, passed down the throne of Iran from father to son from 1265 to 1304, erasing the ephemeral reigns of their juniors. Although true Mongols and faithful to their traditions, they surrounded themselves with learned Persians and, named Darius, Khores, and Alexander, they promoted the renaissance of Iranian nationalism. Below: Family ties are beautifully expressed in this painting, which shows Abaqa crowned and mounted on a horse, riding toward Arghun, on foot holding the child Ghazan, who is sheltered under a parasol, a sign of royal privilege.

The Chagatai and the Timurid empire

Muslim pressure was no less great in the khanate of Chagatai with its uncertain and fluctuating borders, but they tried to resist it. Composed of two very different regions—the north, nomadic, pagan, poor, and devoted to the *Yasaq* of Genghis Khan; the south, sedentary, Muslim, rich, and nourished by one of the oldest cultures in the world—Chagatai was torn by the divergence of interests, culture, and ideas, and by the reciprocal hatred between the territories. It was in vain that a prince like Kebek (1320–1326) tried to maintain cohesion. Sogdiana seceded in 1334, and the real power—now in the hands of Turkic noblity and its most brilliant representative, Emir Qazghan—took shelter behind a series of puppet khans.

In order to reconquer the land, the putative Chagataite Tughluq Timur (1347–1363) had no choice but to convert to Islam. In 1360 he crossed the Syr Darya, chased out or won over the Turkic emirs, and departed, leaving one of his advisors, Timur the Lame—Tamerlane—in charge as suzerain. Under the nominal authority of a bogus

Tamerlane (1336–1405), who wanted to reconstruct the Mongol Empire in its entirety, was an even greater source of inspiration for the West than Genghis Khan (above, a drawing by the Dutch painter Rembrandt). Despite his successes Tamerlane could not maintain his domination over the conquered countries.

In a ride worthy of the Mongols, Tamerlane crisscrossed the globe from India to Russia to the Mediterranean, sowing devastation and ruin. He vanquished the greatest princes of his time—like his success against the Ottoman Beyazid I in Ankara in 1402—and basked in the glow of his victories in Europe, but his campaigns were always in vain. His greatest claim to glory is to have adorned Samarkand with splendid monuments (opposite, bottom, his tomb Gur-e Amir from 1405) and to have given his heirs a taste for science, literature, and art. It was under their reigns that the Timurid renaissance flourished, bringing with it astronomers of genius like Ulugh Beg, poets and memoirists like the emperor Babur, and the great art school of Herat, pictured here with a work by the Persian artist Behzad (left, one of Behzad's most famous paintings, the construction of the castle of Khawaranaq). The joy of life expressed itself in all sorts of ways, as much in the path of the most pure mystique as that of the most impure vices: pederasty, drugs, gambling, and alcoholism.

Mongol khan, Tamerlane modestly proclaimed himself Grand Emir of Bactra in 1370. From Samarkand, where he established his capital, he launched in his turn the conquest of the world. He did not really succeed in his aim, but traveled all over in a spectacular ride vanquishing the strongest and accumulating ruins. He didn't construct anything, apart from a beautiful and dazzling Iranian kingdom, the Timurid renaissance, which was destined to last for better or worse until 1500 and the arrival of the Uzbeks, who were descended from Shayban, son of Jöchi and grandson of Genghis Khan. They created Uzbekistan out of Sogdiana. As for the Chagatai steppes, they sank slowly into decay.

The lovely longevity of the Golden Horde

As in the Chagatai the Mongols who led the Golden
Horde quickly became Turkicized and, like Iran, they
turned to Islam early on, first briefly under the reign of
Berke (1256–1266), then definitively under that of Özbeg
(1312–1340). Masters of Russian principalities, which they
sometimes governed from a distance but with an iron
hand, they decided after the insurrection of Tver' in 1327
that these territories had to provide their own security
and entrusted the execution of these wishes to Moscow,
an event that laid the foundation for the city's future
grandeur. The Horde, despite its cities, remained essentially an itinerant culture and the nomads suffered,
sometimes from their restlessness but always from the
endemic sickness that they could not manage to contain:
the Kipchaks sold each other as slaves, most notably to
the Egyptian Mamluks. The region suffered from a
veritable human hemorrhage and lived in a climate of
perpetual insecurity.

In addition to this condition, the epidemic of the great
plague struck with full force in 1348, overcoming all of
western Asia. The Italians from the Crimean trading
posts helped to spread it in western Europe. The imperial
family were not the only ones who had turned crazy; the
khans fought over power, and there were fourteen of
them between 1360 and 1380.

The Russians dared to rouse themselves against the
Mongols. They had thought themselves free of Mongol
tutelage when they won victory over Kulikovo (1380)
and then again in 1391 when Tamerlane attacked the
Horde. But they had to wait for their liberation,
which had the effect of uniting them. In fact, the
Kipchaks had received a mortal blow and were
soon to disintegrate. The tribes had always
been independent, obeyed no one, and often
created brilliant leaders like Nogai and
Mamai, but around 1430 the khanate of
Crimea split off, followed by Kazan in
1445 and Astrakhan around 1464. The
Mongols were no longer. Some khanates
that descended from the Golden Horde
still had a few good years left and they

Russia's cruelly vindic-
tive war of liberation
against those whom they
called "Tartars" inspired
poets, painters, engravers,
novelists, and filmmakers
(below, the taking of
Kazan in *Ivan the Terrible*
by Sergei Eisenstein,
1943–1946).

occasionally made a show of force, but they were incapable of agreement and of presenting a united front, and were no longer able now to resist the Russians. From 1475, on the khanate of Crimea was obliged to accept the protection of Constantinople in order to survive. Its vassalage only prolonged its existence. The Ottoman empire declined, beaten by the Russians. In 1783 the Turks were forced to abandon Crimea, and they eventually executed the last khan, Shahin Girei, for high treason—a rather mediocre venegeance. By this date, the khanates of Kazan and Astrakhan had long disappeared. Ivan the Terrible (Ivan IV) had captured the former in 1552 and the latter in 1555. The last sovereign of Astrakhan, Yar

The 1380 battle of Kulikovo, which took place near the Don River—and earned the name Donskoi for its victor Dmitry, Duke of Moscow—did not put an end to the Mongol domination of the Russians but showed them that their masters could be beaten. Above: Fifty years after this memorable and celebrated day, the Horde began to break apart, and Kazan, Astrakhan, and the Crimea seceded. Despite this it managed to hold onto its power for a long time. They went on to crush the Muscovites in 1521 and reestablish their vassalage, but this was to be their swan song. The Golden Horde truly stopped existing when the khan of Crimea overtook its capital, Sarai, in 1502. Ivan IV, or Ivan the Terrible (1533–1584), put an end to its two successors by seizing Kazan and Astrakhan.

Muhammad, who had taken refuge with the Uzbeks, founded the Janid or Astrakhanid dynasty in Bukhara (1599–1785). Through it and its successors, the Mangit, the last descendants of Genghis Khan would reign in central Asia until the Bolshevik Revolution. When they

B elow: Mongols often fought among themselves. When Kublai was proclaimed Grand Khan in 1260, his brother Arigböge took up arms

were toppled in 1920, it would be exactly 700 years since Genghis Khan had entered into Bukhara as conqueror.

Khanate against khanate

"If we had remained unified, we would have conquered all the world," the leader Berke is said to have uttered. The Mongols, however, did not remain as one. The khanates fought among themselves. The Golden Horde and the Chagatai fought for the possession of Khwarezm, and each of them fought with the Il-khans. A complicated network of alliances took shape: on the one hand, and without great success, stood the Iranians, Armenians, Crusaders, and Western sovereigns; on the other hand were the more successful ties between the Golden Horde and the Mamluks of Egypt, many of whom descended from the Kipchaks. The attacks by the Golden Horde on the Il-khans over the last half of the 13th century explains the defeat by the Genghis-khanites in their reconquest of Syria in 1299. Internal fighting among the House of Chagatai explains in part their repeated failures against

against him. In the west the battle between the Il-khans of Iran and the Golden Horde began in 1262. All of central Asia was in insurrection by 1277. These fratricidal combats were without a doubt the cause of the general stoppage of conquests, certainly those in India, central Europe, and Syria. Their contemporaries were fully aware of these events for better or worse.

India from 1290 to 1304. This also brings to mind the long conflict between the Ögödeids and the Yüan, which lasted from 1260 to around 1306.

But the Mongol Empire profoundly marked the world. Regardless of whether it had been ephemeral in Iran and in China or a durable regime among the Kipchaks, it played an equally important role in matters great and small in those lands. In China the center of gravity shifted to the north and Peking replaced Xi'an and Nanjing. The Yün-nan would be integrated into the world of the Han. The Chinese would claim domination over Mongolia, Manchuria, Tibet, Xinjiang, and Indochina because these countries had come under the rule of the Yüan. Art and philosophy were enriched and renewed. Foreign religions like Christianity, Manichaeanism, and Buddhism—long protected by the Mongols in the name of religious liberty—would be persecuted.

The khanate of Bukhara, where the last Genghis-khanite princes ruled, was separated from the rest of the world by the great expanse of steppes, deserts, and mountains. It was made even more remote by the will of the powers who saw it as a protective zone between Iran, Russia, and the British empire of India. The region remained in total isolation, making it, like Tibet, one of the most forbidden and most mysterious places in the world. Travelers ventured going there at the risk of their lives. For a long time it maintained its remarkable culture and creative energy, legacies of its past glory. Even in its deepest decay, Bukhara displayed the luxurious and the superb (left, its penultimate emir). Nevertheless it lost Fergana when a rival khanate installed themselves in Kokand around 1700, and was finally obliged to seek the protection of the Russians in 1866.

"Our descendants will attire themselves in golden garments, will eat sweet and rich delicacies, will ride splendid steed, will hold in their arms the loveliest of women, and will forget that they owe these things to us," the Persian historian Rashid ad-Din supposedly said to Genghis Khan. The Mongols never forgot, and the memory that they maintained of Genghis Khan contrasted with the relatively reduced interest he aroused in the West. It was not until the second half of the 20th century that cinema would pay attention (opposite, John Wayne in *The Conqueror*, 1956; this page, bottom, Orson Welles in *The Black Rose*, 1950). From the 16th century on in Mongolia, the founder of the empire had his sanctuary in Edjenkhoro (today in Inner Mongolia or Nei Monggol) and, even though the communist regime was clearly not favorable toward him, celebrations marked his 800th anniversary in 1955. Since the collapse of the Soviet regime, Mongolia has not stopped honoring him with an incredible fervor. This page, top: Contemporary photograph of a modern young woman walking in front of a poster bearing his image is just one piece of evidence among a hundred others.

Left: Despite urbanization, a still rudimentary industrialization, and the development of agriculture, the Mongols lived under a regime that wanted to be modern and was hostile to nomadism, but they remained attached to the patterns of ancestral life. The collapse of Communism freed them to relive the past. Like the dominant ideologies of Buddhism, Genghiskhanism, and nomadism, their traditions and costumes are being rediscovered. The *del*, a unisex costume that is no longer seen except in isolated regions, is regaining popularity in the cities among both upper and lower classes of society. On holidays soldiers dress up as 13th-century warriors. Starting in 1992, the *tug*, the medieval standard with a yak or horse's tail, was officially presented to the army. Buddhist temples reopened, and to be faithful to ancient tolerance, they appeal to Christian missionaries. Nomadism returned to livestock farming and, on the steppes, yurt villages are being built as residences and as vacation homes.

In the Near East, Islam had been subjugated, humiliated, offset by Christianity, and its very existence menaced. Islam, which seemed lost, exacted a stunning revenge, and Christians, who were known for being collaborators, would lose the relative tranquillity they had enjoyed since the Arab conquest. The Turks, whose growing power had already been weakened by the First Crusade, were stopped in their march toward the west, and when they regained their strength, the balance of power was in the process of tipping in favor of Europe. The Mamluks, arrayed with the immense prestige of having been the only ones to vanquish the Mongols on the battlefield and to have subsequently resisted them, would restore Egypt to a splendor almost equal to that of antiquity.

In Europe there was the decline of Hungary, which had been on the way to becoming a great power; there was the colonization of a depopulated Silesia by the Germans, and the continuation of the vassalage of Russia. Later, the imprint left behind by the Mongols would be noticeable in many of the characteristics of the Soviet regime. There was, above all, the desire to reopen the route to the Far East, which was now closed, or to find another one, giving birth to the great discoverers Christopher Columbus and Ferdinand Magellan.

Above: A descendant of Tamerlane from his father's side, and of Genghis Khan from his mother's, Babur Shah (1483–1530) conquered India and founded the great Mughal empire, a reference to the feats of his illustrious ancestor.

The unrivaled empire

The Mongol Empire was one of the great eras of history. Dethroned and pushed back to their steppes, the Mongols attempted it again in the 16th century at a time when the nomad began to be offside, when horses and bows were not enough to win battles. Others would succeed in their place to a certain degree, but no one would re-create what the Mongols had accomplished. First, there was the reign of Tamerlane (1370–1405) and later his descendants the Timurids, who under other skies in India founded an empire bearing their name, that of the Great Mughals, which Queen Victoria of England would inherit. Then there were the Manchus, who, before conquering China and establishing the last imperial dynasty there—the Ch'ing—turned first to the Mongols in order to obtain from them the legitimacy of the Genghis-khanite dynasty (1634). The great-grandsons of the conqueror of the world accorded it to them in hopes of regaining, through this alliance, some of their former grandeur. Instead they drew from it a bondage that would subsume and nearly extinguish them.

Below: Like their ancestors the Timurid princes of central Asia, the great Mughals of India loved gardens and made the construction of mausoleums a major art. Uniting their two passions, they erected splendid funerary palaces within wooded and flowering gardens carved by canals. The 17th-century Taj Mahal in Agra, made of white marble and decorated with carvings of remarkable finesse, was built in a period called "the reign of women" in honor of Mumtaz Mahal, the wife of Jahan Shah (1627–1658). It is the most famous Islamic mausoleum and a masterpiece of world architecture.

DOCUMENTS

With the nomads of the steppes

"I tell you assuredly that if your peasants—without speaking of kings and knights—would march like the Tatar kings and content themselves with the same food, they could conquer the whole world."

William of Rubruck
Travels to the Mongol Empire

The art of nomadism

The Franciscan friar William of Rubruck (c. 1215–c. 1295) was sent by Saint Louis (Louis IX) to Mongolia. In this letter written to the king of France in 1255, he was one of the first to show that nomadism was not disorganized wandering.

They have in no place any settled city to live in, neither do they know where their next will be. They have divided all Scythia among themselves, which stretches from the river Danube to the rising of the sun. And every captain, according to the great or small number of his people, knows the bound of his pastures, and where he ought to feed his cattle, winter and summer, spring and autumn. In the winter they descend into warm regions southward. And in the summer they ascend to the cold regions northward. In winter when snow falls upon the ground, they feed their cattle upon pastures without water, because then they use snow instead of water.

William of Rubruck
Travels to the Mongol Empire

Page 112: Modern stele with an image of Genghis Khan from Ulan Bator, Republic of Mongolia; page 113: The *Kirghiz* in *Jami al-Tawarikh* by Rashid ad-Din, 14th century.

The Mongols were horsemen, but when it came to moving their homes they used camels and wagons. These carts offered the nomads the advantage of being able to move their tents—yurts—without disassembling them.

The matrons make for themselves most beautiful carts, which I am not able to describe unto your Majesty but by pictures only: for I would right willingly have painted all things for you, had my skill been in that direction. A single rich Moal (Mongol), or Tartar, has two hundred or one hundred such carts with chests…. One woman will guide twenty or thirty carts at once, for their country is very flat, and they bind the carts with camels or oxen, one behind another. And there sits a wench in the foremost cart driving the oxen, and all the residue follow on a like pace. When they chance to come to a bad place, they let them loose, and guide them over one by one. They go at a slow pace, as fast as a lamb or an ox might walk. On the next day we met with the carts of Scacatai [Chagatai] laden with houses, and I thought that a mighty city came to meet me. I wondered also at the huge droves of oxen, and horses, and at the flocks of sheep.

Rubruck, *op. cit.*

From antiquity to the present day, the home of the nomads of central Asia has been a sort of tent called a yurt by the Russians. In his description of them Rubruck also discusses the family idols or "ongon."

Their houses in which they sleep, they base upon a round frame of wickers interlaced compactly: the roof consists of wickers, meeting above into one little roundell, out of which ascends a neck like a chimney, which they cover with white felt, and oftentimes they lay mortar or white earth upon the said felt, with the powder of bones, that it may shine white. And sometimes also they cover it with black felt. The felt on the collar they decorate with various beautiful pictures. Before the door they hang a felt curiously painted with vines, trees, birds, and beasts. These houses they make so large that they are often thirty feet in breadth. Measuring once the breadth between the wheel-ruts of one of their carts, I found it to be twenty feet over: and when the house was upon the cart, it stretched over the wheels on each side five feet at least. I counted twenty-two oxen in one team, drawing a house upon a cart, eleven in one order according to the breadth of the cart, and eleven more before them: the axletree of the cart was of huge size, like the mast of a ship. And a fellow stood in the door of the house, upon the forestall of the cart, driving the oxen…. Having taken down their houses from their carts, and turned the doors southward, they place the bed of the master of the house at the north side. The women's place is always on the east side, namely, on the left hand of the master of the house, sitting upon his bed with his face southwards; but the men's place is upon the west side, namely, at the right hand of their master. Men, when they enter the house, will not in any case hang their bows on the women's side. Over the master's head is always an image, like a puppet, made of felt, which they call the master's brother: and another over the head of the good wife or mistress, which they call her brother, is fastened to the wall: and higher up between both of them, there is a little lean one, which is as it were the guardian of the whole house. The mistress of the house places aloft at her bed's feet, on the right hand, a goat-skin stuffed with wool or some other material, and near that a little image or puppet looking towards the maidens and women. Next to the door, also on the women's side, there is another image with a cow's udder, for the women that milk the cows. It is the duty of their women to milk cows. On the other side of the door, next to the men, there is another image with the udder of a mare, for the men milk the mares.

Rubruck, *op. cit.*

The hunt—between necessity and pleasure

Contributing in no small way to their diet, the hunt—always a winter activity—was also a great diversion for the nomads. The Persian historian Juvaini (1226–1283) describes its practical aspects with precision and underscores the "ecological" care taken not to exhaust a species.

He [Genghis Khan] paid great attention to the chase and used to say that the hunting of wild beasts was a proper occupation for the commanders of armies…. For when the Mongols wish to go a-hunting, they first send out scouts to ascertain what kinds of game are available and whether it is scarce or abundant…. Whenever the Khan sets out on the great hunt (which takes place at the beginning of the winter season)…the right wing, left wing and centre of the army are drawn up…. For a month, or two, or three they form a hunting ring and drive the game slowly and gradually before them, taking care lest any escape from the ring…. For two or three months, by day and by night, they drive the game in this manner, like a flock of sheep, and dispatch messages to the Khan to inform him of the condition…. Finally, when the ring has been con-tracted to a diameter of two or three parasangs, they bind ropes together and cast felts over them; while the troops come to a halt all around the ring, standing shoulder to shoulder…. First the Khan rides in together with some of his retinue; then, after he has wearied of the sport, they dismount upon high ground in the centre of the *nerge* to watch the princes likewise entering the ring, and after them, in due order, the *noyans*, the commanders and the troops. Several days pass in this manner; then, when nothing is left of the game but a few wounded and emaciated stragglers, old men and greybeards humbly approach the Khan, offer up prayers for his well-being and intercede for the lives of the remaining animals asking that they be suffered to depart to some place nearer to grass and water…. A friend has related how during the reign of Qa'an they were hunting one winter in this fashion and Qa'an, in order to view the scene, had seated himself upon a hilltop; where-

upon beasts of every kind set their faces towards his throne and from the foot of the hill set up a wailing and lamentation like that of petitioners for justice. Qa'an commanded that they should be set free and the hand of injury withheld from them…. Now war—with its killing, counting of the slain and sparing of the survivors—is after the same fashion, and indeed analogous in every detail.

'Ala-ad-Din 'Ata-Malik Juvaini
*Genghis Khan: The History
of the World Conqueror*

Frugality

Great drinkers and willing drunks, the Mongols and the Turkic people showed when necessary an extreme frugality to which the contemporary observers often accorded their victories. "Their food," said Carpini, "consists of anything they can put in their mouths. In effect they eat dogs, wolves, foxes, and horses, and if needed, human flesh." Marco Polo (1254–1324) was more verbose.

They are stout fighters, excelling in courage and hardihood. Let me explain how it is that they can endure more than any other men. Often enough, if need be, they will go or stay for a whole month without provisions, drinking only the milk of a mare and eating wild game of their own taking. Their horses, meanwhile, support themselves by graz-ing, so that there is no need to carry barley or straw…. They are of all men in the world the best able to endure exertion and hardship and the least costly to maintain and therefore the best adapted for conquering territory and overthrowing kingdoms.

Marco Polo
The Description of the World

The role of women

Among the nomads of the steppes, women enjoyed great freedom and an elevated status. The Moroccan traveler and good conservative Muslim Ibn Battuta (1304–1377) was indignant about the situation.

A remarkable thing which I saw in this country [the Golden Horde] was the respect shown to women by the Turks, for they hold a more dignified position than the men.… I saw the wife of the amír in her waggon. The entire waggon

Engraving by Nitschmann of an encampment of yurts.

was covered with rich blue woollen cloth, and the windows and doors of the tent were open. With the princess were four maidens, exquisitely beautiful and richly dressed, and behind her were a number of waggons with maidens belonging to her suite. When she came near the amír's camp she alighted with about thirty of the maidens who carried her train…and she walked in this stately manner. When she reached the amír he rose before her and greeted her and sat her beside him, with the maidens standing round her. Skins of *qumizz* [koumiss, the fermented mare's milk] were brought and she, pouring some into a cup, knelt before him and gave it to him, afterwards pouring out

a cup for his brother. Then the amír poured out a cup for her and food was brought in and she ate with him.… I saw also the wives of the merchants and commonalty. One of them will sit in a waggon which is being drawn by horses.… The windows of the tent are open and her face is visible, for the Turkish women do not veil themselves. Sometimes a woman will be accompanied by her husband and anyone seeing him would take him for one of her servants.

Ibn Battuta
Travels in Asia and Africa 1325–1354

The high status of women was also underscored, but with less indignation, by other travelers, including the Franciscan friars Giovanni da Pian del Carpini in 1246–1247 and Ricold de Monte Croce around 1271.

Girls and women ride and gallop on horses as skillfully as men. We even saw them carrying quivers and bows.… The Tartar women make everything: skin clothes, shoes, leggings, and everything made of leather. They drive carts and repair them, they load camels, and are quick and vigorous in all their tasks.

Giovanni da Pian del Carpini
The Story of the Mongols Whom We Call the Tartars

The Tartars hold all the women of the world in high esteem but theirs above all. It is they who control public and domestic matters, who sells and who buys. They are proud and bellicose. They ride like men, and I have often seen them enter cities armed with a bow and arrows like men. They are very faithful to their husbands.

Ricold de Monte Croce
Peregrinations

Religion

The Mongol religion, which was also that of the ancient Turks, was founded on the belief in a single God—heaven [or tängri]—whose power manifested itself through multiple secondary divinities and by the magical and mystical means of shamanism, involving trances, a relationship with the spirits, divination, magical healing, and cosmic voyages. In addition, the Mongols showed the greatest tolerance, lavished privileges on priests of all faiths, and guarded against denominational conflicts; in return, they demanded that others pray for them.

Faith

His expression of faith is spread throughout the text, but Rubruck summarized it in these words spoken by the Grand Khan Mangu:

"We Moals [Mongols]…we believe there is but one God, by whom we live and by whom we die, and we have for him an upright heart…. Even as God has given several fingers to the hand, so has he given man several ways."

William of Rubruck, *op. cit.*

Shamanism

Shamanism enjoyed a great authority. Rubruck noted it and pointed out the various aspects of this religion that came under its control.

Their soothsayers, as [the khan] himself said, were their priests, and all they command to be done, is executed immediately…. They are numerous and they have a superior, who is like a pontiff…. He predicts the eclipses of the sun and of the moon…. They predict the lucky and unlucky days for all circumstances of life. Also, war is never declared nor battles waged without their advice…. These arrange to pass over fire all that is sent to the court…. They also purify with fire all furniture left by the dead…. The soothsayers are also called in at the birth of a child, to foretell his fate, and when some one falls ill…. The soothsayers disturbed the atmosphere by their incantations.

Rubruck further provided one of the first descriptions of a shamanic séance.

Some of these soothsayers evoke demons. They assemble, at night, in their house those who wish to have answers from the devil; they put cooked meat in the centre of the dwelling, and the *cham* [shaman] who invokes begins by saying mysterious words, and, holding a drum in his hand, he strikes it hard on the ground. Then he passes into a fury and they bind him. Then the devil appears in the midst of the darkness; the *cham* gives him this meat to eat and commands his answers.

William of Rubruck, *op. cit.*

The great shaman Kökchü, called "the most holy" (Teb-Tenggeri), played an important role in Genghis Khan's coronation, then tried to reign through him. Genghis Khan took advantage of a quarrel and, surmounting his fear, had him put to death. The imperial Annals relate the episode this way:

Odčigin, pulling Teb Tenggeri, went out, the three strongmen which beforetime had been ready between the threshold of the door having, in the face of him, seized Teb Tenggeri, pulling him, going out, breaking his back asunder, casting him unto the extremity of the row of carts of the left side…. Činggis Qahan [Genghis Khan] seeing that, having broken his backbone, one had cast Teb Tenggeri unto the extremity of the row of carts, making one to bring a gray tent from behind, making one to place it over Teb Tenggeri, saying, "Harness the harnessings. We shall journey," he journeyed from thence. When, having covered the hole at the top of the tent in which one had place Teb and having stopped its door, one had caused people to watch over it, the third night, at the moment when the brightness of day was yellow, he opened the hole at the top of the tent and came out together with his body. When one examined, it was established that verily it was Teb at its place there. When Činggis Qahan [Genghis Khan] spake, he said, "Because Teb Tenggeri had laid hand upon my younger brethren and because to sow discord among them he had uttered among my younger brethren a slander without fundament, he was no more loved by Heaven, and his life, together with his body, was carried away."
The Secret History of the Mongols

Cults

Prayers to the mountain spirit were one of the Mongols' principal cults. The Secret History *recounts how Genghis Khan hid one day in the Burqan Qaldun (the Kentei Mountains, or the Hentiyn Nuruu of today) and declared:*

"Every morning I shall sacrifice unto Mount Burqan. Every day I shall pray unto it. Let the seed of my seed observe this," over against the sun he hanged his girdle on his neck, hanged his hat in his hand, struck his hand into his breast, and, kneeling nine times toward the sun, offered a sprinkling of mare's milk and a prayer.
The Secret History of the Mongols, op. cit.

Chingiz-Khan went up alone to the summit of a hill, bared his head, turned his face towards the earth and for three days and nights offered up prayer…. Thereupon he descended from the hill…making ready for war.
Juvaini, *op. cit.*

When the two armies drew close to each other [in Hungary] Batu went up on to a hilltop; and for one day and night he spoke to no one but prayed and lamented.
Juvaini, *op. cit.*

Before drinking, the Mongols would make offerings to their idols and to the various powers of the universe.

And when they come together to drink and make merry, they sprinkle part of their drink upon the image which is above the master's head: afterward upon other images in order: then a servant goes out of the house with a cup full of drink sprinkling it three times towards the south, and bowing his knee at every time: and this is done for the honour of the fire. Then he performs the same towards the east, for the honour of the air: and then to the west for the honour of the water: and lastly to the north in behalf of the dead.

When the master holds a cup in his hand to drink, before he drinks he pours part upon the ground. If he drinks sitting on horseback, he pours out part upon the neck or mane of his horse. After the servant has so discharged his cups to the four quarters of the world, he returns into the house: and two other servants stand ready with two cups, and two basins, to carry drink to their master and his wife.

William of Rubruck, op. cit.

The afterlife

In a few words Carpini defined the Mongols' faith in the afterlife.

They believe, however, that after death they live in another world, that flocks multiply, that they shall eat and drink and do other things which living men do in this world.

Carpini, op. cit.

The site of a tomb might be kept secret or might be marked by a mound, a structure, or a stone statue.

The Comans of the Golden Horde build a great tomb over their dead, and erect the image with his face towards the east, holding a drinking cup in his hand, at the height of his navel.

William of Rubruck, op. cit.

Aside from his excellent information about funerals, Ricold also provides one of the most unusual descriptions of burial rites, which are still practiced in modern times.

The Tartars believe and hope in a kind of vague resurrection based on the image of the life they know. Each person provides for his dead according to his resources. The poor cook meat in abundance and bury it with the dead whom they surround with sustenance and also with new clothes, in addition to the ones the dead person already wears. They also add a little bit of money. The rich, in addition to the meat and the money, provide another change of clothing and place on the head of the dead person a rolled-up precious article of clothing…. The great nobles add a good horse to all these items. While the others are preparing to bury the dead master, his equerry mounts his horse and tires it by racing it in every direction until it is completely exhausted. Then he washes the head of the horse with a strong and pure wine. The horse falls dead. He guts it and, in the space now emptied of its entrails, he fills the stomach with fresh grasses. Then he pushes a stake in from the rear that comes out through the mouth. He leaves it impaled like that and suspends the horse so that it is always ready for the moment when the master will come to ride it. Then they cover the dead with a sepulcher. When an emperor dies, they add precious stones and even great treasures to all these items. Their custom is even to bury up to twenty living slaves and servants with the dead master so that they will be ready to serve him in the afterlife.

Ricold, op. cit.

Tolerance

Being the adherent of no religion and the follower of no creed, he [Genghis Khan] eschewed bigotry, and the preference of one faith to another, and the placing of some above others; rather he honoured and respected the learned and pious of every sect…. And as he viewed the Moslems with the eye of respect, so also did he hold the Christians and [Buddhist] idolaters in high esteem. As for his children and grandchildren, several of them have chosen a religion according to their inclination, some adopting Islam, others embracing Christianity, others selecting idolatry and others again cleaving to the ancient canon of their fathers and forefathers…. But though they have adopted some religion they still for the most part avoid all show of fanaticism and do not swerve from the *yasa* of Chingiz-Khan, namely, to consider all sects as one and not to distinguish them from one another.

Juvaini, *op. cit.*

Dozens of edicts regarding tolerance were issued in China and in the Golden Horde in favor of priests and religious communities. They all refer, more or less, to the ones promulgated by Genghis Khan for his friend Ch'ang-ch'un and Taoism.

The following is forbidden to bureaucrats everywhere: regarding all religious structures and in those habitations where they follow the Way (Tao) and those who are dependent on the solitary divine Kieou, these are all men who spend their days reading holy books and invoking God. These are the people who ask for the emperor a longevity of ten thousand times ten thousand years. It is why I forbid that all requisitions and all taxes, large or small, be applied to them.

Edouard Chavannes
"*Inscriptions and Pieces de chancellerie chinoises de l'époque mongole*"
(*Inscriptions and Documents from the Chinese Ministry in the Mongol Era*)
In *T'oung Pao,* 1904

Around 1325 Odoric of Pordenone (1265–1331) described a most revealing ceremony in the religious life of the Mongol Empire that took place in Peking (now Beijing) on the return of the Khan to his capital.

He related that once upon a time, when the Great Khan was on his journey from Sandu to Cambalech, [Peking], he (Friar Odoric), with four other Minor Friars, was sitting under the shade of a tree by the side of the road along which the Khan was about to pass. And one of the brethren was a bishop. So when the Khan began to draw near, the bishop put on his episcopal robes and took a cross and fastened it to the end of a staff, so as to raise it aloft; and then those four began to chant with loud voices the hymn, *Veni Creator Spiritus*! And then the Great Khan, hearing the sound thereof, asked what it meant. And those four barons who go beside him replied that it was four of the Frank Rabbans (i.e., of the Christian monks). So the Khan called them to him, and the bishop thereupon taking the cross from the staff presented it to the Khan to kiss. Now at the time he was lying down, but as soon as he saw the cross he sat up, and doffing the cap that he wore, kissed the cross in the most reverent and humble manner.

The Travels of Friar Odoric: A 14th-Century Journal of the Blessed Odoric of Pordenone

The Grand Khan

The Mongol emperors were descended from heaven; they were its "sons" in the Chinese manner. The Secret History of the Mongols *recounts their origin through two myths. The first is set in ancient times and concerns the ancestors of this people, while the second focuses more directly on Genghis Khan. Almost all of the contemporary writers, regardless of their nationality, reported it more or less faithfully. The stories have not been forgotten today.*

Here is how the Armenian historian Kirakos (1201–1207) transcribed them.

The Mongols repeated that their sovereign was the equal of God…. To prove it they maintained that Genghis Khan had not been begotten by the seed of a man but that a light coming from an invisible place had entered through the roof of his mother's home and had said to her, "Conceive and you will have a son who will be sovereign of the world."

One morning at the moment when day was breaking, she was sleeping until she was awoken by a luminous ray that penetrated into her tent by the opening at the top. She clearly saw a man with a white face and with deep blue eyes come out of this ray of light and descend towards her…. This man approached her very gently, placed himself next to her on her bed and observed the rights of a husband. Then he departed leaving through the same opening…. This man came again five to six days after and continued thus his visits from time to time. However from the first night Alan Qo'a carried in her breast the pledge of that union.

"They kept watch over the home." One time one of the guards saw a brilliant ray like that of the sun descend into the tent of Alan Qo'a through the top opening. He quickly awoke his companions. Some of them could only see the ray penetrating into the tent, but all of them saw it leave a little later without being able however to recognize a human form in this ray of light.

Kirakos, in Dulaurier's *"Les Mongols d'après les documents arméniens"* (The Mongols According to Armenian Documents) *Journal Asiatique,* 1858

The universal monarchy

Being born of heaven, the khan was therefore destined to unify the whole world under his law. The grand Mongol shaman affirmed this destiny at Genghis Khan's enthronement.

At this time there arose a man of whom I have heard from trustworthy Mongols that during the severe cold that prevails in those regions he used to walk naked through the desert and the mountains and then to return and say:

"God has spoken with me and has said: 'I have given all the face of the earth to Temüjin and his children and named him Chingiz-Khan.'" They called this person Teb-Tengri ["Most Heavenly"], and whatever he said Chingiz-Khan used implicitly to follow.

Juvaini, *op. cit.*

The Mongols clearly proclaimed their sovereign will everywhere and none could ignore it.

The Tartars mean to conquer the entire world if they can, as we have already said. This is why their emperor heads his letters thus: "The Power of God, the Emperor of all Men" and the superscription of his seal is this: "God in Heaven and Cuyuc Khan over the Earth, the Power of God, the Seal of the Emperor of all Men."

Carpini, *op. cit.*

The enthronement

Even though the monarchy was hereditary, the khans were selected from the imperial family by a general assembly of nobles, the khuriltai. *The enthronement of the sovereign was a spectacular ceremony. Carpini assisted in Güyük's coronation.*

Then we entered the land of the Mongols whom we call the Tartars.... We rushed along the entire road because this was our Tartars' order and they quickly led us to the High Council which had gathered now for several years for the election of the emperor.... Outside there were Duke Ierozlai of Russian Suzdal and many Kytai and Solangi dukes and two of the sons of the King of Georgia, the ambassador of the Caliph of Baghdad who was a sultan, and more than ten other Saracen sultans.... Indeed there were more than four thousand ambassadors among them who brought tribute and gifts, and sultans and other dukes who came to submit as well as those whom the Tartars had sent for and those who are governors of territories...every time that Cuyuc left the tent and so he was hailed by pretty virgins in scarlet wool clothes. They bowed to him, which was not done to any other leader however long he waited outside. They called this the Sira Horde. We left there and everyone rode together to another place about three or four leagues away where there was another tent prepared in a beautiful plain next to a river between hills, which they call the golden horde, where Cuyuc was to be enthroned on the day of the Assumption of Our Lord.... When they had done this a long while they returned to the tent and placed Cuyuc on the imperial throne and the leaders knelt to him in public and after this all the people knelt, except we who were not his subjects. They then began to drink and, as their custom is, they drank continuously until evening.... There were so many gifts given, in silk, in samite, rich cloth and silken cloth and silken belts worked with gold, rich furs and other gifts that it was wonderful to see.... More than fifty wagons were placed beyond a hill a long way from the camp and they were all filled with gold and silver and silk clothing which were divided between the emperor and his nobles. And the nobles individually divided their share between their men as it pleased them.

Carpini, *op. cit.*

The conquest of the world

The physical annihilation of those who resisted their weapons was the first means employed by the Mongols to assure their universal domination. Their very well organized propaganda spread the most sinister reports, sometimes exaggerated or false and even of cannibalism, which added to the expanding terror of their destruction. They preferred, however, that people rally to them freely, as did the Uighurs, for example. Consequently, they did not handle diplomatic advances very well as attested to in the numerous letters sent to the papacy and to Western sovereigns, most notably to the French king.

Massacres and destruction

Order of Genghis Khan: Whoever presumed to oppose and resist him, that man, in enforcement of the *yasas* and ordinances which he imposed, he utterly destroyed, together with all his followers, children, partisans, armies, lands and territories.

Juvaini, *op. cit.*

A quarrel, which gave no respite, was discharged from the town [Bamiyan] and hit a son of Chaghatai, the favourite grandchild of Chingiz-Khan. The Mongols made the greater haste to capture the town, and when it was taken Chingiz-Khan gave orders that every living creature, from mankind down to the brute beasts, should be killed; that no prisoner should be taken; that not even the child in its mother's womb should be spared.

Juvaini, *op. cit.*

When these people had been defeated the Tartars advanced against Russia and devastated it. They destroyed cities and castles and killed men and besieged Kiev, which is the greatest Russian city, and after a long siege they took Kiev and killed the townspeople, so when we went through that country we found countless human skulls and bones from the dead scattered over the field. Indeed Kiev had been a very great and populous city but now is reduced to almost nothing. In fact, there are hardly two hundred houses there now and the people are held in the strictest servitude.

Carpini, *op. cit.*

15 December, 1237, the Tatars laid siege to Riazan. Its defenders held out for six days. On the seventh the city fell. Half of the population had their throats cut, the other half were burned alive. Prince Yuri Igorevich was put to death. The city and the lands of Riazan were overwhelmed. Their glory disappeared and in its place one could no longer see anything but smoke, earth, and ashes.

Grekov and Iakoubovski
La Horde d'Or (*The Golden Horde*)

The desired end was achieved.

They spread such horror in all regions of the East that in several cities the mere fear created by their names was sufficient to make pregnant women miscarry.

Ricold, *op. cit.*

Paralyzed by fear people no longer sought to resist. Ibn al-Athir (d. 1234) wrote:

It is related, for example, that a single Tatar horseman rode into a densely populated village and began killing the inhabitants one after the other, without anyone trying to defend himself. I have heard that one Tatar, having no weapon on him and wishing to kill someone whom he had taken prisoner, ordered the man to lie down on the ground, then went and fetched a sword and slew the wretch, who had not stirred.

He reports what one of his friends told him:

"I was on the road with seventeen others; we saw a Tatar horseman arrive who told us to tie each other's hands behind our backs. My companions began to obey him, and I said to them: 'This man is alone; we must kill him and run away,' 'We're too frightened,' they answered. I then urged them: 'But this man is going to kill you. Let us kill him! It may be that Allah will save us.' But upon my soul not one of them dared to do it. So I stabbed him to death with my knife, and we fled to safety."

Ibn al-Athir, in René Grousset's
*The Empire of the Steppes:
A History of Central Asia*

Horrifying portraits

The terror born at the time of the great Mongol invasions created horrifying portraits of these people and their country, which were spread more by hearsayers than by actual witnesses. The Western chronicles, which were particularly dramatic, seemed copied from those written at the time of the invasion of the Huns in the mid-4th century AD. Hyon de Narbonnes wrote to the archbishop of Bordeaux:

Their leaders feed on cadavers like it was bread and leave to the vultures only bones…. Old and ugly women were given to these cannibals…to serve as their nourishment during the day. As for those who were pretty, they abstained from eating them but, despite their cries and their lamentations, they smothered them under multitudes of violations that they made them submit to…. They sullied virgins until they gave up the ghost, then cutting off their breasts that they reserved for their chiefs as a delicacy, they dined on the remains with gluttony.

Speaking not from hearsay but from experience, the medieval travelers were less hysterical. Carpini noted:

Their appearance is quite different from that of everyone else. Tartars have eyes and cheeks wider apart than other men. Their cheeks stick out a good deal from the jaw and they have a flat middle-sized nose and small eyes and eyelids raised to the eyebrows.

Carpini, *op. cit.*

And Ricold de Monte Croce said a few decades later:

When I came among them it seemed truly to me as if I had entered another world. We had discovered the horrible and monstrous people, the Tartars. The Tartars differ from all other nations of the world by their looks, their customs, and their rituals. They have a very strong and large face with small eyes like narrow slits cutting across the middle of their faces. They do not have much of a beard to the point that many of them, particularly the old men, resemble monkeys.

Ricold, *op. cit.*

Diplomacy

Diplomatic correspondence by the Mongols evolved greatly between the time of their great expansion, when they behaved arrogantly, and then subsequently after their failures against the Mamluk Egyptians, when they hoped to collaborate with the Franks.

With the power of Eternal Heaven and as universal khan of the great people, hear our words.... You have sent to us a request of submission that we have heard from your ambassadors. And if you would act according to your own words, you, great pope, with the kings would come together and in person to render homage to us and at that time we would make you listen to the orders of the *Yasaq* (the law of Genghis Khan).... With the power of God, from the east of the rising sun to the west, all the lands have been destroyed. Except by order from God, how could someone do this? You must speak with a sincere heart and say we will be your subjects, we will give you our strength. You, in person, at the head of the kings all together and without exception must come to us to offer service and homage. And if you do not observe the order of God and contravene our command, we will consider you our enemies.

Letter from Güyük to
Pope Innocent IV (1246)
Collection of the Vatican

Wherever there are Moals, Naimans, Merkits or Mustelmen, wherever ears can hear, or a horse can travel, there you will hear and understand it. My orders will be heard and understood and believed and those who do will not want war to be waged against us, and those who heed and make war against us shall see though they have eyes and see not, and when they shall want to hold anything, they shall be without hands; such is the order of God eternal. By the eternal virtue of God, through the great world of the Moals, the order of Mangu Khan is sent to the lord of the French, King Louis, and to all the other lords, and to the priests and to the great realm of the French, to understand our words. And the order of the eternal God has become the order of Chinghis Khan [Genghis Khan], and since Chinghis Khan or others after him, this order has not reached you.... We, therefore, are sending you the written order of the eternal God, by your above-named priests, the order of the eternal God that we are making you understand. And when you shall have received and believed it, if you want to obey us, you will send us your ambassadors, and you will thus let us know if you wish to be at peace or at war with us. When, by the power of the eternal God, from the rising of the sun to the west, the whole world shall be united in joy and in peace, thus shall it be known what we are to be. If you have heard and understood the order of the eternal God, and if you resist it, saying: "Our land is far away, our mountains are high and many, our sea is big," and, in this, believe that you may declare war against us, the eternal God knows that we know what we can do. He makes easy that which is difficult, and brings closer together that which is separated by distance.

Letter from the Grand Khan Mangu to Saint Louis (around 1253–1254), in William of Rubruck, *op. cit.*

God spoke to our ancestor Genghis Khan by the voice of Teb-tenggeri [the shaman Kökchü] saying, "I have put you at the head of these peoples and of realms and I have made you the king of the entire world...." In bringing to your understanding the aforesaid revelation, we make you know that we will fulfill the message that the living God has entrusted to us with more certitude that you will consider and with more care since our power was conferred by the Eternal Heaven himself. So that the rumor does not spread that we have written in vain, we will show you with a brief résumé the number of evils which have befallen those who recently did not accept the truth of our mission or rather that it was conferred to us by the living God.

Letter from Hülegü to Saint Louis (1260) In P. Meyvaert, "An Unknown Letter of Hülegü Il-Khan of Persia to King Louis IX," in *Viator*, 1980

By the power of the eternal Heaven and under the auspices of the grand Khan [Kublai], this is our word: King of France, we propose to you to leave on campaign the last day of the last month of winter in the year of the panther [January 1291] and to camp before Damascus around the 15th of the first month of spring. If you will send from your side troops at the arranged time, we will retake Jerusalem and we will give it to you. But it is useless to make our troops march if you will miss the rendezvous.

Letter from Arghun to Philip the Good (1289) National Archives of France

Siege of a Middle Eastern fortress.

The marvels of the world

As time went on and the menace lessened and the terror was forgotten, the vision of the West changed. The Mongol peace allowed for intercontinental voyages and, with them, the discovery of an unimagined world through increased commercial and missionary travel. Everything became a subject for astonishment and marvel. The khans were portrayed as heroes, and the Far East was described as the most beautiful, the richest, the most prestigious land of the world.

What to believe?

The travelers' tales were studded with incredible descriptions, and sorting them out is difficult when there are so many unknown things.

Charcoal

It is a fact that throughout the province of Cathay there is a sort of black stone, which is dug out of veins in the hillsides and burns like logs. These stones keep a fire going better than wood. I assure you that, if you put them on the fire in the evening and see that they are well alight, they will continue to burn all night, so that you will find them still glowing in the morning. They do not give off flames, except a little when they are first kindled, just as charcoal does, and once they have caught fire they give out great heat…. So these stones, being very plentiful and very cheap, effect a great saving of wood.

Marco Polo, *op. cit.*

The raining rocks

The people of the steppes possessed a stone (yai, yada tash) from which rain fell. They used it mostly in war but it happened that it turned against them.

Ulugh-Noyan commanded him to begin practising his art and ordered the whole army to put on raincoats over their winter clothes and not to dismount from their horses for three days and nights. The Qanqli [magician] busied himself with his *yai* so that it began to rain behind the Mongols, and on the last day the rain was changed to snow, to which was added a cold wind. From this excessive summer chill, which was such as they had not experienced in winter, the Khitayan [Chinese] army were disheartened.

Juvaini, *op. cit.*

Skis

There are also three Oengai [people] who attach to their feet polished bones and glide like that over ice or frozen snow, with such rapidity that they catch birds and beasts.

William of Rubruck, *op. cit.*

Paper money

The ordinary money of Cathay is a paper made of cotton the length and breadth of a palm, stamped with lines similar to those of the seal of Mangu Khan. The Cathayans write with a brush like painters use, and a single figure comprises several letters, signifies a word.

William of Rubruck, *op. cit.*

We note that on the same occasion the Franciscan gave the first description of Chinese writing.

You must know that he has money made for him by the following process, out of the bark of trees—to be

P age from the manuscript *Cadeau fait aux observateurs traitant de curieux offertes par les villes et des merveilles rencontrées dans les voyages* (*Gift given to the observers dealing with the curious offerings of cities and with the marvels encountered in their travels*), 1356.

precise, from mulberry trees…. The fine bast between the bark and the wood of the tree is stripped off. Then it is crumbled and pounded and flattened out with the aid of glue into sheets like sheets of cotton paper, which are all black. When made, they are cut up into rectangles of various sizes, longer than they are broad. The smallest is worth half a small tornesel; the next an entire such tornesel…. And all these papers are sealed with the seal of the Great Khan…. And then the money is authentic.

Marco Polo, *op. cit.*

Serpents

In this province live huge snakes and serpents of such a size that no one could help being amazed even to hear of them. They are loathsome creatures to behold…. You may take it for a fact that there are some of them ten paces in length that are as thick as a stout cask…. They have two squat legs in front near the head…. Their mouth is big enough to swallow a man at one gulp. Their teeth are huge.

Marco Polo, *op. cit.*

Elephants

These animals are extraordinary. By their size, by their weight, by their strength, and even by their intelligence, they surpass all other animals on earth. This animal has a huge head with tiny eyes (smaller than that of a horse), ears in the form of the wings of an owl or a bat, a nose which, being born at the top of its head, descends all the way to the ground, two exterior teeth pointing out in front of a size, a thickness, and a length that are far from normal…. They have huge feet, fitted with six nails that resemble the feet of an ox or even more of a camel. This animal can transport on its back, in a sort of wooden cabin, more than thirty men.

Jourdain Catalani de Séverac
Les Merveilles de l'Asie
(*The Marvels of Asia*)

Yaks

There are many wild cattle here, as big as elephants and very handsome in appearance; for they are covered with long hair, except on the back, and are white and black in colour. The length of their hair is fully three palms.

Marco Polo, *op. cit.*

Rocs (the fabulous birds of the Arabs)

They are so big that they rise with the ease of an elephant in the air. I myself encountered someone who said he'd seen one of them whose single wing reached twenty-four palms in length.

Jourdain de Séverac, *op. cit.*

Dwarves

In the east of Cathay there are very high rocks where live certain creatures who have the form of a human being, except they cannot bend knees. Also, they move about, I do not know just how, but by jumping. They are not more than a cubit tall and their body is all covered with hair. These beings live in inaccessible caverns. The hunters bring them mead to get them drunk…. The jumping creatures come out of their caves, taste this mead, and cry: "*Chin, chin.*"

William of Rubruck, *op. cit.*

These Pygmies are three spans in height…. And the full-sized men who dwell there beget sons who are more than half of them like those Pygmies who are so small. The women are wedded in their fifth year, and so there are born and begotten of these little people a countless number.

Odoric of Pordenone, *op. cit.*

Monsters

But as the Tartars crossed a wasteland they discovered certain monsters (as was told to us for certain), who had only one arm and hand in the middle of the chest and one foot and so that two of them shot as one person with a single bow, and they ran so fast that horses could not catch them. They ran jumping on this one foot and when they tired of going that way they would go on hand and foot revolving as in a circle.

Carpini, *op. cit.*

Dog men

The king recounted to us many marvelous and unknown things that he had seen and heard in the barbarian nations. He said…that there was a country where the women are reasonable in the manner of men and the men are without reason and look like dogs, large and covered with hair…. These dogs hunt and live off the proceeds with their women. From their union are born male children who are in the shape of dogs while the girls are in the form of women.

Hayton, *La Flore des estoires de la terre d'Orient,*
In *Recueil des historiens des Croisades (Anthology of the History of the Crusades)*
Paris, 1869

An "extreme" hospitality

I give you my word that if a stranger comes to a house here to seek hospitality he receives a very warm welcome. The host bids his wife do everything that the guest wishes. Then he leaves the house and goes about his own business and stays away two or three days. Meanwhile the guest stays with his wife in the house and does what he will with her, lying with her in one bed just as if she were his own wife; and they lead a gay life together.

Marco Polo, *op. cit.*

Extraordinary cities

The great Chinese cities, rich and crowded, are one of the favorite subjects of the travelers.

Khanbalik, the city of the Khan: Peking

Here the Great Khan hath his residence, and hath a great palace, the walls of which are some four miles in compass. And within this space be many other fine palaces. [For within the great palace wall is a second enclosure, with a distance between them of perhaps half a bowshot, and in the midst between those two walls are kept his stores and all his slaves; whilst within the inner enclosure dwells the Great Khan with all his family, who are most numerous, so many sons and daughters, sons-in-law, and grandchildren hath he....] And within the enclosure of the great palace there hath been a hill thrown up on which another palace is built, the most beautiful in the whole world. And this whole hill is planted over with trees, wherefrom it hath the name of the *Green Mount*. And at the side of this hill hath been formed a lake [more than a mile round], and a most beautiful bridge built across it. And on this lake there be such multitudes of wild geese and ducks and swans, that it is something to wonder at; so that there is no need for that lord to go from home when he wisheth for sport. Also within the walls are thickets full of sundry sorts of wild animals; so that he can follow the chase when he chooses without ever quitting the domain.... But when the Lord Khan is seated on his imperial throne, the queen is placed at his left hand; and a step lower are two others of his women; whilst at the bottom of the steps stand all the other ladies of his family.... On the right hand of the king is placed his firstborn son that shall reign after him; and below stand all who are of the blood royal.

Odoric of Pordenone, *op. cit.*

Quinsay: Hangzhou

Then he reaches the splendid city of Kinsai, whose name means "City of Heaven." It well merits a description, because it is without doubt the finest and most splendid city in the world.... First, then, it was stated that the city of Kinsai is about 100 miles in circumference, because its streets and watercourses are wide and spacious. Then there are market-places, which because of the multitudes that throng them must be very large and spacious.... And in each of these squares, three days in the week, there is a gathering of forty to fifty thousand people, who come to market bringing everything that could be desired to sustain life.... The houses in general are very solidly built and richly decorated. The inhabitants take such delight in ornaments, paintings, and elaborations that the amount spent on them is something staggering. The natives of Kinsai are men of peace, through being so cosseted and pampered by their kings, who were of the same temper. They have no skill in handling arms and do not keep any in their houses. There is prevalent among them a dislike and distaste for strife or any sort of disagreement. They pursue their trades and handicrafts with great diligence and honesty.... They are no less kind to foreigners who come to their city for trade. They entertain them in their houses with cordial hospitality and are generous of help and advice in the business they have to do.

Marco Polo, *op. cit.*

The judgment of history

The attitudes of the Chinese, Muslims, Russians, and other people toward the Mongols depends on the reactions by contemporary observers to the events, but it is surprising to discover that, along with the violent diatribes, there are many praises for the conquerors. Later on the Europeans reacted in a less uniform manner. French political philosopher Montesquieu and Russians like the writer Pushkin and historian Nikolai Karamzin, along with 20th-century historians René Grousset and Joachim Barckhausen, held divergent opinions.

The Tatars had nothing in common with the Moors. Although they conquered Russia, they gave it neither algebra nor Aristotle.

Aleksandr Pushkin

To conquer for a master

The peoples of northern Europe have conquered as free men; the people of northern Asia have conquered as slaves and have been victorious only for a master.... This is why the genius of the Tartars...has always been similar to that of the empires of Asia. The peoples in the latter are governed by the cudgel; the Tartar peoples, by the lash...what the peoples of Asia have always called punishment, the peoples of Europe have always called gross offence. When the Tartars destroyed the Greek empire, they established servitude and despotism in the conquered countries; when the Goths conquered the Roman empire, they founded monarchy and liberty everywhere.

Charles-Louis de Secondat,
Baron de Montesquieu
L'Esprit des lois (*The Spirit of the Laws*)
Book XVII, 5, 1748

Even more barbarous...

The invasion of Batu overwhelmed Russia. The last spark of light was very nearly snuffed out. By some good fortune, it was not extinguished. But a new order of life began, a painful order for humanity on first examination, but a more careful observation reveals, in effect, a cause for good in the evil and, in the destruction itself, a benefit for the whole. The shadow of barbarism that obscured the horizon of Russia hid Europe from us at the moment when useful science and positive practices spread more and more [throughout the continent]. In this era Russia, tortured by the Mongols, pooled its energy for one aim only—not to disappear. The nature of the Russians today still carries the ignoble mark imprinted there by the Mongol barbarians.

Nikolai M. Karamzin
(1766–1826)
Histoire de l'État russe
(*History of the Russian State*)
Paris 1819–1828

"A levelheaded spirit, a fair leader"

The paradox of Jenghiz-Khanite history lies in the contrast between the wise, reflective, and moral character of a leader who regulated his own conduct and that of his people by maxims of sound common sense and well-established justice and the brutal reactions of a people newly emerged from primitive savagery, who sought no other means than those of terror for the subjugation of their enemies—a people for whom human life had no value whatever and who, as nomads, lacked all conception of the life of sedentary peoples, of urban conditions or farming culture, or of anything alien to their native steppe. The modern historian's astonishment is basically the same as that of Rashid ad-Din or the compilers of the *Yüan Shih* when confronted by this perfectly natural blend of wisdom—even moderation—in the leader and of ferocity in upbringing, in atavistic reversions, and in tribal traditions.

Grousset, *op. cit.*

"One of those men who make history"

Perhaps the route to power pursued by Genghis Khan seemed for so long like an act of bravado against reason or like a miracle that we only consider the external circumstances and the apparent equilibrium of powers. However, he was as logical and calculating as the next man, and he operated only within the realm of the possible and based his plans on that reality.

He was almost without power and without means when he began, and he forged his race of masters from the poorest of the earth.... There was neither an army nor an apparatus of state awaiting him. He created them out of nothing.

Genghis Khan was certainly one of those men—perhaps the greatest—who made history. But he could only become it because History created him. He acknowledged this role by trying to understand it and play it, by subordinating himself to it, by serving it.... His power was nourished by the deep roots of his background because he was not a usurper without a tradition and History lived on through in him.... Traditions and dreams were the possibilities of his brilliant politics and he made them into realities.

The Mongols were renewed by him. Over the course of five generations they occupied a historic place. For a century and a half the fate of the world was in their hands. An adventurous odyssey led them halfway around the world, only to lead them back to their point of departure weighed down by their only glory. Once again they inhabited their felt tents.... They recounted how marvelous was the world they had lost. The grand past was now just a dream. Once again the Mongols were poor nomads like their ancient ancestors had been.

Joachim Barckhausen
L'Empire jaune de Gengis Khan
(*The Yellow Empire of Genghis Khan*)
Paris, 1935

Timeline

c. 1155 Birth of Temüjin (Genghis Khan).

1164 Engaged to Börte. Death of Yesügei, father of Temüjin, assassinated by the Tatars.

c. 1181 Marriage of Temüjin and Börte. Kidnapping of Börte.

1182 Birth of Jöchi, first son of Temüjin.

1184 Birth of Chagatai, his second son.

1186 Birth of Ögödei, his third son.

1193 Birth of Tolui, his fourth son.

c. 1195–1196 Temüjin is proclaimed khan.

1202 Genghis Khan defeats the Tatars and dominates all of eastern, then central, Mongolia.

1206 Genghis Khan proclaimed emperor.

1206–1209 Campaign against the Tangut (Hsi-Hsia).

1208 Birth of Mangu, oldest son of Tolui.

1209 The Uighurs rally to Genghis Khan.

1211 Beginning of the Chinese campaign against the Jin. Alliance with the Nestorian Önguts.

1212 Jebe, Mongol general, takes Liao-yang. The Khitans join Genghis Khan.

1215 Capture of Peking. Occupation of Manchuria.

1217 Genghis Khan leaves China, leaving the command of the troops to his lieutenant Muqali.

1219 Genghis Khan concentrates his forces against Khwarezm and penetrates Sogdiana.

1220 Bukhara and Samarkand captured.

1221 Occupation of Bactra (Balkh). Death of Mutugen, grandson of Genghis Khan, near Bamiyan. Genghis Khan at the Indus River.

1223 Promulgation of the first edict of tolerance. Genghis Khan has a horsing accident.

1225 Genghis Khan returns to Mongolia. Second horsing accident.

1227 Death of Genghis Khan.

1229 Ögödei elected Grand Khan.

1230–1231 Mongols destroy the forces of Khwarezm. Occupation of Iran.

1231–1236 New campaign in Korea. Taking of T'ang-kouen in the north of China. Death of Tolui in 1232.

1235 Foundation of Karakorum, capital of the Mongols in Mongolia. Declaration of war against the Sung (South China).

1236 Taking of Tch'eng-tou. Third campaign in Korea. Invasion of Georgia. Beginning of the campaign in Europe.

1237 Submission of the Kipchak territories. Entry of the Mongols into Russia. Storming of Riazan and Kolomna. Capture of Isfahan.

1238 Capture of Moscow and Vladimir. Incursions into Iraq.

1239 Annexation of Armenia.

1240 Taking of Kiev.

1241 The Mongols cross

the Vistula River. Taking of Kraków, Buda (Budapest). Peace with Korea. Death of Ögödei. Batu crosses the Danube and takes Gran in Hungary and Zagreb in Croatia.

1242 Batu evacuates Hungary and installs himself at the north of the Black Sea. Death of Chagatai. Taking of Erzurum (eastern Anatolia).

1242–1246 Regency of Töregene.

1243 Invasion of Anatolia. Defeat of the Seljuks, who became vassals of the Mongols.

1244 Vassalage of Little Armenia. King Hayton, also known as Hethum, inaugurates a policy of collaboration with the Mongols.

1245–1247 Carpini travels to Mongolia.

1247 Resumption of hostilities with Korea.

1248 Death of Güyük. The Mongols reach the Adriatic.

1250 Foundation of Sarai.

1251 Mangu is elected Grand Khan.

1253 The Mongols occupy the Yün-nan.

1253–1255 Voyage by William of Rubruck to Mongolia.

1254–1255 Voyage of King Hayton of Armenia to Karakorum.

1255 Death of Batu.

1256 Berke takes over as head of the Golden Horde. A *khuriltai* reopens the war against the Sung. Hülegü becomes viceroy of

Iran. Alamut is captured. Destruction of the Assassins.

1257 Capitulation of Korea. Invasion of Iraq. Attacks on India.

1258 Mongol offensive in Indochina. Mangu leaves for China. Taking of Baghdad. Execution of the Abbasid caliph. Annexation of Iraq.

1259 Death of Mangu.

1260 Kublai is proclaimed Grand Khan in China and establishes his residence in Peking. Arigböge is proclaimed Grand Khan in Mongolia. Beginning of the schism of the empire. Destruction of Mongol forces at Ain Jalut.

1262 First conflict between the Il-khans of Iran and the Golden Horde in the Caucasus.

1263 Alliance of the Mamluks and the Mongols of the Golden Horde against the Il-khans.

1264 Arigböge surrenders to his brother Kublai.

1265 Death of Hülegü. Coronation of Abaqa in Iran.

1266 Death of Berke.

1269 Alliance between the Golden Horde and the houses of the Ögödeids and the Chagataids.

1274 The Mongols attempt to land in Japan.

1275 War of Kublai against Qaidu.

1275 Taking of Hangchou.

1277 The Mamluks defeat the Mongols at Elbistan. The Mongols reinforce their control of Anatolia.

1280 The Mongols, masters of all of China, assume the name of Yüan and establish a dynasty.

1281 Beginning of the war against Champa (now Vietnam). Second attempt of launch against Japan. Attack by the Il-khans on Syria.

1282 Death of Il-khan Abaqa.

1286–1287 Mongol campaign in Annam.

1287 Mongols pillage Pagan, capital of Burma. Qaidu succeeds in forming an alliance against Kublai.

1288 Indochina is subjugated. Kublai defeats the alliance in Manchuria.

1291 Death of the Il-khan Arghun. Gaikhatu succeeds him.

1294 Death of Kublai. Oljäi Temür succeeds him.

1295 Ghazan is elected Il-khan. Attacks on India.

1299 Attack by Ghazan on Syria. Capture of Aleppo and Damascus.

1302 End of the Seljuk sultanate of Anatolia.

1303 Last Mongolian intervention in Syria.

1305 Mongol invasions in Kashmir.

1307 Death of the Grand Khan Oljäi Temür.

1316 Death of the Il-khan Öljeitü.

1317 Reign of Abu Sa'id.

1322–1329 Odoric of Pordenone in Peking.

1327 Mongol expedition in India.

1328 Death of Grand Khan Yisun Temür.

1333 Coronation of the last (Yüan) Grand Khan Toghan Temür.

1334 Schism of the Chagatai khanate. Sogdiana secedes.

1336 Death of Abu Sa'id. Collapse of Mongol power in Iran.

1340 Death of Özbeg, khan of the Golden Horde.

1369 Mongols are expelled from China. Debut of the Ming dynasty.

1370 Tamerlane is proclaimed Grand Emir and establishes his capital in Samarkand.

1380 Battle of Kulikovo.

1389 Tamerlane attacks the Golden Horde.

1405 Death of Tamerlane.

1430 Foundation of the khanate of Crimea.

1445 Foundation of the khanate of Kazan.

1464 Foundation of the khanate of Astrakhan.

1502 End of the Golden Horde.

1525 Babur Shah establishes the Mughal empire in India.

1552 Capture of Kazan by the Russians.

1555 Capture of Astrakhan by the Russians.

1858 End of the Mughal empire.

1920 With the Soviet revolution, the last royal heirs of Genghis Khan disappear.

Further Reading

CLASSIC TEXTS

Carpini, G., *The Story of the Mongols Whom We Call the Tartars*, 1996

Cleaves, F.W., transl., *The Secret History of the Mongols*, 1982

Ibn Battuta, *Travels in Asia and Africa 1325–1354*, 2001

John of Joinville, *The Life of St. Louis*, 1955

Juvaini, A., *Genghis Khan: The History of the World Conqueror*, 1997

Odoric of Pordenone, *The Travels of Friar Odoric*, 2002

Polo, M., *The Travels of Marco Polo*, 1958 (translated by Ronald Latham)

Rashid ad-Din, *The Successors of Genghis Khan*, 1971

Rubruck, W., *The Journey of William of Rubruck to the Eastern Parts of the World, 1253–55*, 1988

CONTEMPORARY STUDIES

Boyle, J.A., *The Mongol World Empire*, 1977

Carboni, S., *Legacy of Genghis Khan: Courtly Art and Culture in Western Asia 1256–1353*, 2002

Chambers, J., *The Devil's Horsemen: The Mongol Invasion of Europe*, 1979

Grousset, R., *The Empire of the Steppes: A History of Central Asia*, 1970

Halperin, C.J., *Russia and the Golden Horde*, 1987

Irwin, R., *Islamic Art in Context*, 1997

Lister, R.P., *Genghis Khan*, 2000

Morgan, D., *The Mongols*, 1986

Rossabi, M., *Khubilai Khan: His Life and Times*, 1988

Roux, J.-P., *Histoire de l'empire mongol* (*History of the Mongol Empire*), 1993

———, *L'Asie centrale: Histoire et civilisations* (*Central Asia: Its History and Civilizations*), 1997

———, *Histoire des Turcs* (*History of the Turks*), 2000

Spence, J.D., *The Chan's Great Continent: China in Western Minds*, 1998

Spuler, B., *History of the Mongols: Based on Eastern and Western Accounts of the 13th and 14th Centuries*, 1989

Stewart, S., *In the Empire of Genghis Khan: An Amazing Odyssey Through the Lands of the Most-Feared Conqueror in History*, 2002

List of Illustrations

O**pposite:** The birth of Ghazan in *Jami al-Tawarikh* by Rashid ad-Din, 14th century.

Index

The departure of Odoric of Pordenone, in *Romances and Travel*, 14th century.

Photograph Credits

Text Credits

Jean-Paul Roux, a historian of Asia, is the honorary
director of research at the French National Center for
Scientific Research (CNRS) and professor emeritus of
Islamic art at the École du Louvre. He has organized two
major exhibitions on this art and he is the author of,
among other books, *La Religion des Turcs et des Mongols*
(*The Religion of the Turks and the Mongols*) (Payot, 1984;
awarded a prize by the Académie française), *Tamerlan*
(*Tamerlane*) (Fayard, 1991), *Histoire de l'empire mongol*
(*History of the Mongol Empire*) (Fayard, 1993), and
L'Asie centrale: Histoire et civilisations (*Central Asia:
Its History and Civilizations*) (Fayard, 1997).

Translated from the French by Toula Ballas

For Harry N. Abrams, Inc.
Project Manager: Susan Richmond
Editor: Libby Hruska
Typographic designer: Tina Thompson
Cover designer: Brankica Kovrlija
Text permissions: David Savage

Library of Congress Cataloging-in-Publication Data

Roux, Jean-Paul, 1925–
    [Gengis Khan et l'Empire Mongol. English]
    Genghis Khan and the Mongol empire / Jean-Paul Roux.
        p. cm.
    Includes bibliographical references and index.
    ISBN 0-8109-9103-9 (pbk.)
    1. Genghis Khan, 1162–1227. 2. Mongols—Kings and rulers—Biography.
3. Mongols—History—To 1500. I. Title.
DS22 .R68 2003
950'.2'092—dc21

                                              2002151469

Printed and bound in Italy by Editoriale Lloyd, Trieste
10 9 8 7 6 5 4 3 2 1